# THE NEEDLEWORKER'S COLLECTION

## DESIGNS IN

# CROSS STITCH

*Over 40 creative projects and 100 original motifs*

4105
Published in the USA 1996 by JG Press
Distributed by World Publications, Inc.
Copyright © 1996 by CLB Publishing
Godalming, Surrey, UK

Printed and bound in Singapore
ISBN 1-57215-155-2

The JG Press imprint is a trademark of JG Press, Inc.
455 Somerset Avenue, North Dighton, MA 02764

THE NEEDLEWORKER'S COLLECTION

DESIGNS
· IN ·

# CROSS STITCH

*Over 40 creative projects and 100 original motifs*

JG
PRESS

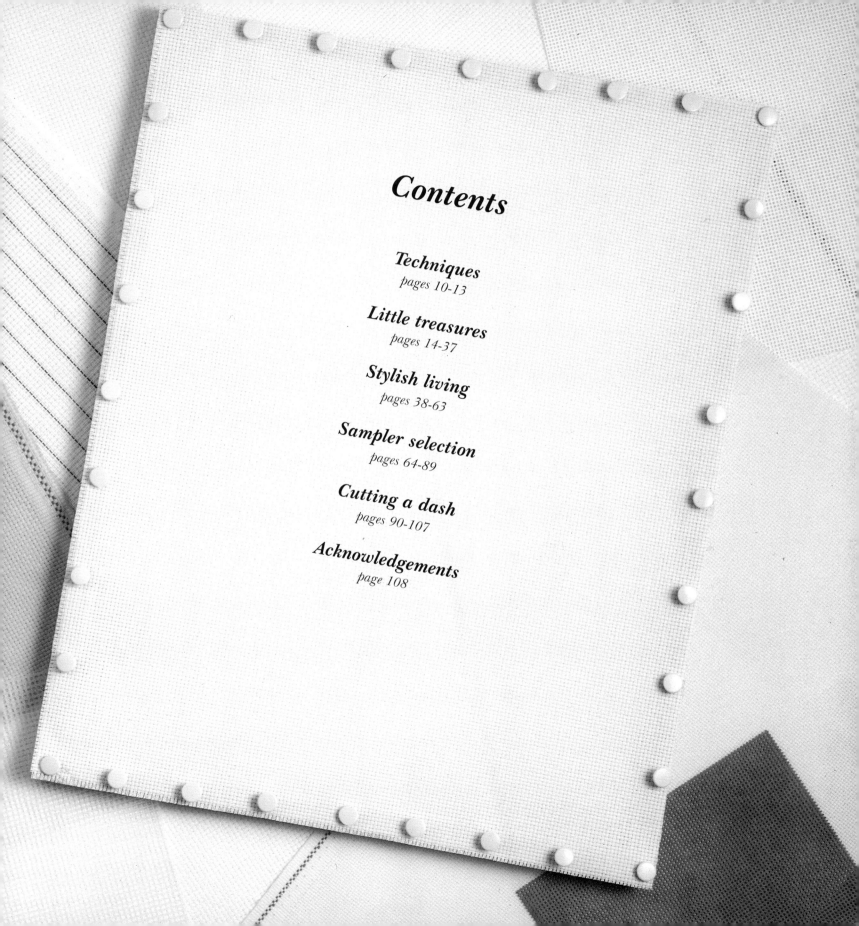

# Contents

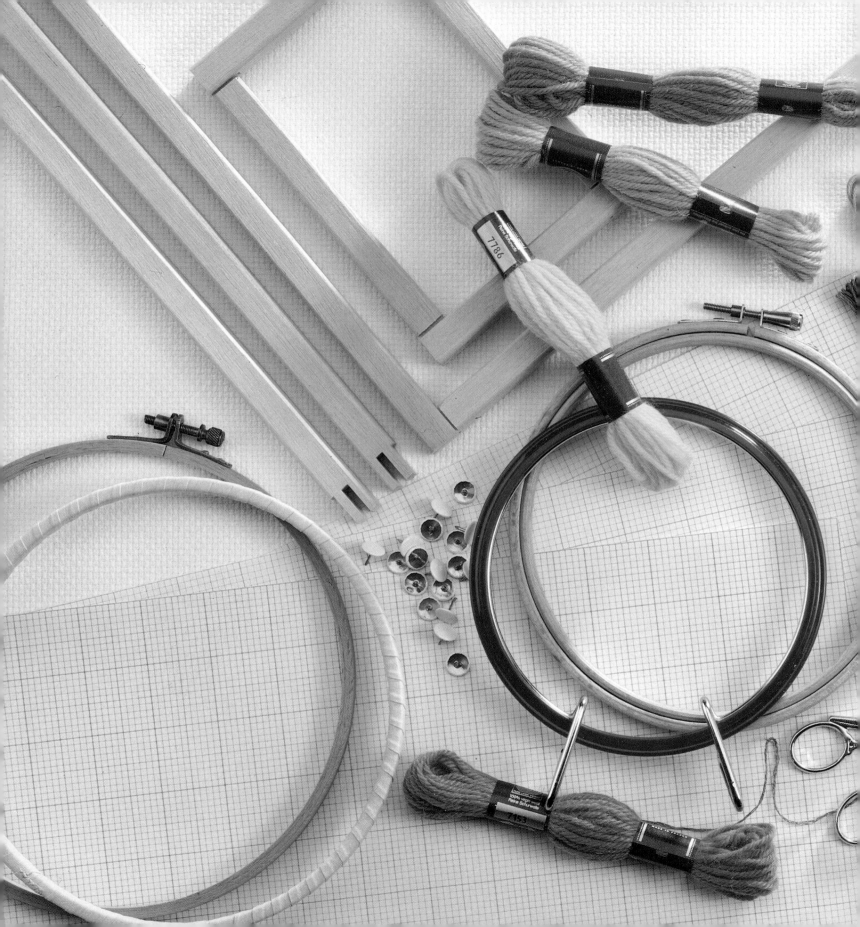

# Techniques

Cross stitch embroidery is easy to work, even for the inexperienced stitcher, and you will quickly become confident working intricate, multi-coloured designs in many colours of thread. Always buy the best quality materials you can afford as this will ensure that your finished embroidery will look better, last longer and launder successfully.

If you are left-handed, the stitch diagrams on the following page will be easier to follow if you prop the book up in front of a mirror, then follow the reflected images.

### FABRIC

Evenweave fabric enables you to work the cross stitch designs neatly and evenly. This fabric has the same number of woven blocks or threads to every 2.5cm (1in). The weight varies; fine fabrics have more blocks to each 2.5cm (1in) than coarse ones. The number of blocks is known as the count.

Many of the projects in this book are worked on an evenweave fabric called Aida. It is available in a wide range of colour shades. The most popular counts are 11 and 14 blocks to 2.5cm (1in).

Perforated paper and plastic canvas are fairly new materials for cross stitch. Perforated paper is available in a limited colour range and has 14 paper 'threads' to every 2.5cm (1in).

Plastic canvas is available in various sizes and can be cut to shape, but all the canvas threads have to be covered by stitching.

### THREADS

All the projects in the book with the exception of the tree decorations on page 60 and the floral band sampler on page 84 have been stitched with stranded cotton (embroidery floss). This is made from six loosely twisted strands so that a length can be split into different weights.

Use your threads in 38cm (15in) lengths to avoid tangling and fraying. Divide lengths of stranded cotton and recombine the strands.

### NEEDLES

Needles are graded from thick (low numbers) to fine (high numbers). Tapestry needles are ideal for cross stitch, since the blunt points slide easily through the material. Useful sizes are 24 and 26.

Crewel needles have long eyes and are useful for working cross stitch by the waste canvas method. A fine crewel needle is useful for applying beads.

### HOOPS AND FRAMES

For all but the smallest designs, mount your fabric in a circular hoop or rectangular frame since this will help you stitch evenly and accurately.

# Techniques

When stitching, avoid making a knot at the end of your thread. Instead, leave about 5cm (2in) of thread loose on the surface of the fabric close to the area you are stitching and darn in the loose ends later. To finish a length of thread, slip the needle under a group of stitches on the wrong side and cut off the loose end.

Each coloured square on the charts represents one complete cross stitch and the heavy lines represent back stitch. The key for each chart show you which colours to use and the project instructions tell you the fabric size and the number of strands of thread to use.

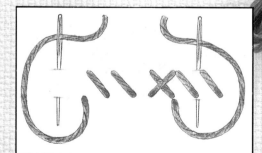

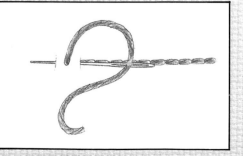

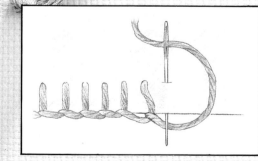

## CROSS STITCH

**Method one**: The first two diagrams show cross stitch worked individually. This produces slightly raised crosses. Complete each cross before proceeding to the next one. Work details and individual stitches by this method.

**Method two**: For large areas, work each row of cross stitch over two journeys. Work a row of diagonal stitches from right to left, then complete the crosses with a second row of diagonal stitches worked in the opposite direction. A row of single diagonal stitches is called half cross stitch.

## BACK STITCH

Work back stitch from right to left, making small, even stitches forwards and backwards along the row. Unless otherwise instructed, keep back stitches of identical size to the cross stitches.

## BLANKET STITCH

Work blanket stitch from left to right, pulling the needle through the fabric over the top of the working thread, as shown in the diagram. Space the stitches at regular intervals along the row.

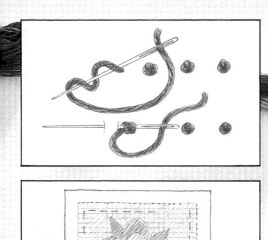

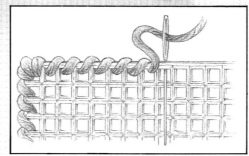

## HOOPS

Bind the smaller hoop, without the screw, with thin cotton tape to help prevent the fabric sagging as you stitch. The tape also helps to prevent damage to delicate fabrics.

Loosen the screw on larger hoop. Spread the fabric, right side up, over the smaller hoop and press larger hoop over. Tighten screw slightly, and manipulate until fabric is evenly stretched. Tighten the screw.

## FRAMES

To use a non-adjustable rectangular frame, first bind the edges of your fabric with strips of masking tape. Slot the frame sides together, then pin the fabric to the frame with drawing pins, taking care to keep the fabric grain straight.

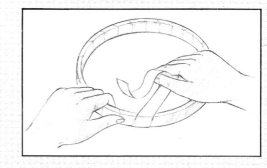

## OVERCAST STITCH

Place two pieces of plastic canvas together with wrong sides facing and line up the matching holes. Work overcast stitch round the edge as shown in the diagram, going through both sets of holes with each stitch. Work three stitches into each corner to cover the canvas edge.

## FRENCH KNOT

**Top**: Bring thread through fabric and hold in the left hand. Twist the needle round the thread. Holding the thread, insert the needle back in the fabric. Pull the thread through to fabric back.

## WASTE CANVAS

**Step 1**: Cut a canvas piece large enough for the design. Tack this on to the fabric and work the design.

**Step 2**: Moisten canvas and pull out canvas threads.

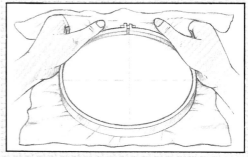

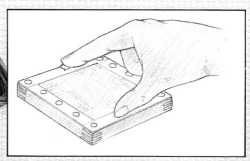

# Little treasures

There is nothing more delightful than giving and receiving
hand-made presents, and with the delicate art of cross stitch
it is easy to make lovely gifts for your favourite
friends and family.
Here is a wonderful selection
with just that in mind,
or use the patterns given to
create your own special presents.

# Jewellery Boxes

### WORKBASKET

❖

Two pieces 15 x 15cm (6 x 6in)
and one piece 20 x 20cm
(8 x 8in) of white 11 count Aida

❖

1 skein of DMC Stranded Cotton in
each of the following colours:
white*, yellow 307, lavender 341,
scarlet 606, grass green 703,
brown 918, turquoise 959, orange
972, kingfisher 995,
airforce blue 3807
*Note - you may omit the white
stitches if you prefer

❖

Tapestry needle size 26

❖

Small embroidery hoop

❖

Tacking thread in a dark colour
and sewing needle

❖

Silver-plated trinket boxes from
Framecraft (page 108) – two boxes
with a 7cm (2³⁄₄in) work area and
one box with a 9cm (3¹⁄₂in ) work
area

❖

Fine-point black felt pen with
permanent ink

COLOUR / BACKSTITCH KEY: MOTH

| BROWN | LAVENDER | KINGFISHER | TURQUOISE | ORANGE |
|---|---|---|---|---|
| 918 | 341 | 996 | 959 | 972 |
| 918 | | 995 | | |

**BUTTERFLIES**        **MOTHS**

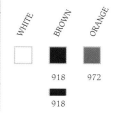

COLOUR / BACKSTITCH KEY: BUMBLE BEE

| WHITE | BROWN | ORANGE |
|---|---|---|
| | 918 | 972 |
| | 918 | |

*Decorate a collection of silver-plated jewellery boxes with repeating patterns of tiny moths, butterflies and bumble bees. The finished boxes will grace your dressing table, keeping treasured jewellery and other trinkets in a safe place.*

COLOUR / BACKSTITCH KEY: BUTTERFLY

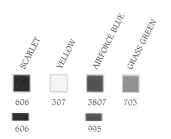

| SCARLET | YELLOW | AIRFORCE BLUE | GRASS GREEN |
|---|---|---|---|
| 606 | 307 | 3807 | 703 |
| 606 | | 995 | |

## PREPARING THE FABRIC

**1** *Place the three pieces of fabric on a flat surface, a table top is ideal, and lay the acetate circle from each trinket box centrally on the fabric. Make sure the largest acetate circle from the 9cm (3¹/₂in) box is positioned on the largest piece of evenweave fabric.*

**2** *Carefully draw around the acetate circles using the felt pen, then remove the acetate circles from the fabric.*

**3** *Work a horizontal and vertical row of tacking stitches inside each drawn circle to mark the centre. This will correspond to the centre on the chart.*

**4** *Mark the centre of each chart with a soft pencil.*

## WORKING THE STITCHES

Mount the fabric in the embroidery hoop (page 13). Beginning at the centre of each piece, work the design in cross stitch (page 12) from the chart using three strands of thread in the tapestry needle.

Each coloured square on the chart represents one complete cross stitch worked over one woven block of fabric.

The half squares on the moth and butterfly charts are filled by working one arm of the cross.

When all the cross stitch areas have been completed, add the linear details from the charts in back stitch (page 12) again using three strands of thread.

## MAKING UP THE BOXES

**1** *Press the finished embroideries lightly on the wrong side with a warm iron. Press each piece over a well-padded surface and take care not to crush the stitches. Leave to cool before mounting them.*

**2** *Cut out each embroidery along the circular outline and mount in the box lids following the manufacturer's instructions. Ensure that the fabric design is central in the lid.*

# Brooch Cushion

## WORKBASKET

❖

Two pieces 25 x 25cm
(10 x 10in) of cream
11 count Aida

❖

1 skein of DMC Stranded Cotton in
each of the following colours:
purple 550, grass green 703,
bluebell blue 799, pine green 911,
yellow 973, pale green 3348,
fuchsia 3608, rose pink 3708,
lavender 3746

❖

Tapestry needle size 26

❖

Embroidery hoop or rectangular
frame

❖

Tacking thread in a dark colour

❖

Matching sewing thread

❖

Sewing needle and pins

❖

Four ready-made dark green
tassels about 8cm
(3¼in) long

❖

75cm (30in) ready-made
dark green piping

❖

White polyester toy stuffing
(available at most good
haberdashery stores)

❖

Knitting needle

**BROOCH CUSHION**

| YELLOW | BLUEBELL BLUE | ROSE PINK | PINE GREEN | PALE GREEN |
|--------|---------------|-----------|------------|------------|
| 973 | 799 | 3708 | 911 | 3348 |

| GRASS GREEN | PURPLE | LAVENDER | FUCHSIA PINK |
|-------------|--------|----------|--------------|
| 703 | 550 | 3746 | 3608 |

## WORKING THE STITCHES

Fold one piece of fabric in four to find the centre and mark with a few tacking stitches. Mark the centre of the chart with a soft pencil. Mount the centre of the fabric in the hoop or frame (page 13).

Work the knot garden design in cross stitch (page 12) from the chart using three strands of thread in the tapestry needle throughout.

Work outwards from the centre of the design, remembering that each coloured square on the chart represents one complete cross stitch worked over one woven block of fabric.

*A formal Elizabethan knot garden with its clipped yew topiary and box hedges, regimented paths and neat beds of herbs and flowers inspired the design for this colourful brooch cushion. Trim the edges with ready-made piping and tassels or add a ruffled lace trim.*

## MAKING UP THE CUSHION

**1** *Press the embroidery lightly, taking care not to crush the stitches. Trim the surplus fabric on the front, allowing a margin of 2.5cm (1in) of unworked fabric. Cut the remaining fabric piece to this size.*

**2** *Tack the piping round the front of the cushion. Align the flat edge of the piping with the raw edge of the fabric and tuck in the ends neatly. Attach a tassel to corner of the cushion. Position the tassels with the loops towards the corners.*

**3** *Place the second piece of fabric over the top with right sides facing. Tack in place, taking care not to catch the tassels in with the tacking. Machine stitch together close to the raised part of the piping, leaving a 10cm (4in) gap for turning.*

**4** *Trim fabric at the corners and turn to the right side. Press, and stuff with stuffing, using a knitting needle to push stuffing into corners. Slipstitch the opening closed.*

**This border (above) could be used as an alternative to the one given on the main chart.**

**Bright colours (right) add a splash of originality to a smaller brooch cushion.**

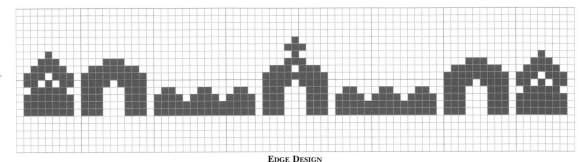

**EDGE DESIGN**

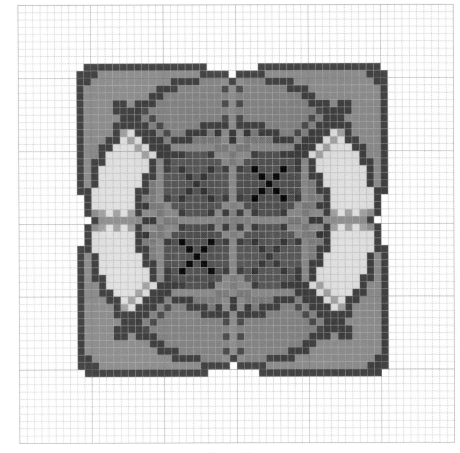

**GARDEN RING**

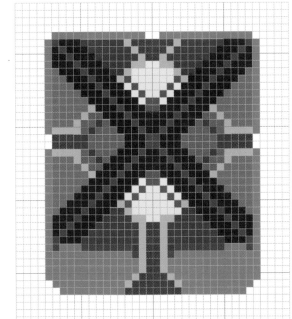

**INSIDE KNOTS**

*An alternative version of an Elizabethan knot garden is given here, worked in a brighter range of colours, offering the same stylish design shapes.*

# Herb Bags

### WORKBASKET

❖

Small pieces of cream 11 count Aida large enough to mount in a hoop

❖

1 skein of DMC Stranded Cotton in each of the following colours: hyacinth 340, fuchsia 3608, forest green 3808, pine green 3818, sage green 3816, mid green 3815

❖

Tapestry needle size 26

❖

Small embroidery hoop and tacking thread in a dark colour

❖

Matching sewing thread

❖

Sewing needle and pins

❖

Six pieces 18 x 28cm (7 x 11in) of natural linen fabric with a woven windowpane check, preferably with a selvedge running across the top of each piece

❖

Green ribbon 1cm (¹/₂in) wide

❖

Fusible bonding web

❖

Knitting needle

❖

Dried kitchen herbs

*Dry home-grown kitchen herbs in your airing cupboard. Store the dried herbs in individual linen bags decorated with embroidered motifs.*

COLOUR/BACKSTITCH KEY:
THYMUS

| GRASS GREEN | FUCHSIA | FOREST GREEN |
|---|---|---|
| 704 | 3608 | 3808 |

22

thymus
vulgaris

salvia
officinalis

rosmarinus
officinalis

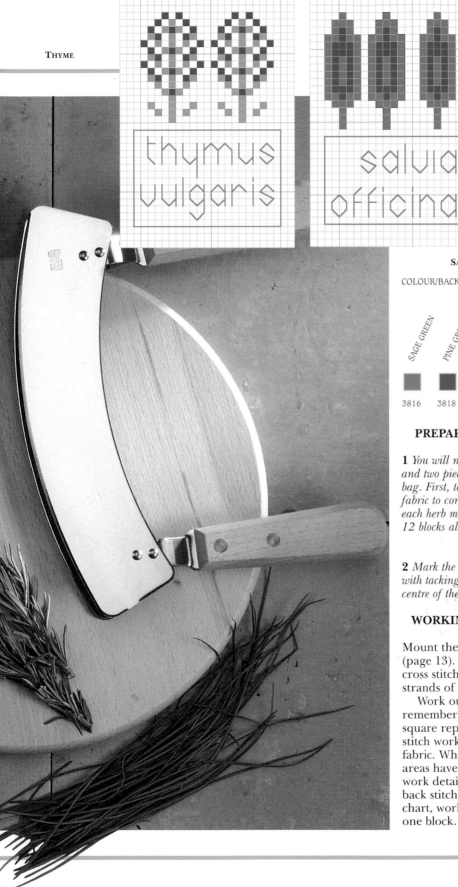

**SAGE**

COLOUR/BACKSTITCH KEY: SALVIA

SAGE GREEN    PINE GRREN    FOREST GREEN

3816    3818    3808

**ROSEMARY**

COLOUR/BACKSTITCH KEY: ROSMARINUS

MID GREEN    HYACINTH    FOREST GREEN

3815    340    3808

### PREPARING THE FABRIC

*1 You will need one piece of fabric and two pieces of linen for each herb bag. First, tack a rectangle on the fabric to correspond with the size of each herb motif, leaving a margin of 12 blocks all round the rectangle.*

*2 Mark the centre of the rectangle with tacking stitches and mark the centre of the chart with a soft pencil.*

### WORKING THE STITCHES

Mount the fabric in the hoop (page 13). Work the design in cross stitch (page 12) using three strands of thread.

    Work out from the centre, remembering that each charted square represents one cross stitch worked over one block of fabric. When all the cross stitch areas have been completed, work details and Latin names in back stitch (page 12) from the chart, working each stitch over one block.

### MAKING UP THE BAGS

*1 Press the embroidery on the wrong side over a well-padded surface. Following the manufacturer's instructions, iron a piece of fusible bonding web on to the back of each embroidery. Cut away the surplus fabric, leaving a margin of six unworked blocks round the design.*

*2 Peel away the backing paper from the motifs and position each one centrally on a piece of linen. Iron the motifs to attach them. Using the tapestry needle, pull out threads from one row of fabric blocks.*

*3 Pin a decorated piece of linen and a plain piece together with right sides facing and machine round three sides, leaving the top open. Trim surplus fabric and turn the bags to the right side, pushing corners out with the knitting needle.*

*4 Press and if there is a selvedge trim the top of each bag. Fill two thirds full with herbs, gather and secure with a ribbon.*

# Celestial Gifts

**WORKBASKET**

✦

60 x 60cm (24 x 24in) white 11 count Aida

✦

1 skein of Anchor Stranded Cotton in each of the following colours: navy 127, royal blue 133, lemon 288, sunshine yellow 291, orange 304

✦

1 spool of Kreinik Metallics Fine (#8) Braid in each of the following colours: silver 001, gold 002, antique gold 221

✦

Tapestry needle size 24

✦

Small embroidery hoop and tacking thread in a dark colour

✦

Sewing needle

✦

Hand-turned circular picture frames – two frames with an 8cm (3¼in) work area and one frame with a 10cm (4in) work area

✦

*Sun, moon and star patterns worked in stranded cotton and highlighted with silver and gold threads decorate a trio of hand-turned wooden frames. The celestial theme is echoed by a group of wooden trinket boxes with embroidered silver and gold patterns mounted in the lids.*

❖

Hand-turned trinket boxes – three boxes with a 3.5cm (1½in) work area and one box with an 8cm (3¼in) work area

❖

Mid blue non-boil fabric dye and cooking salt for fixing the colour

❖

Fine-point black felt pen with permanent ink

## PREPARING THE FABRIC

**1** *Wet the fabric with cold water. Mix up the dye and salt in a suitable container following the manufacturer's instructions and dye the fabric for the recommended time. Rinse the fabric until the water runs clear, then allow to dry.*

**2** *Press the fabric on the wrong side with a hot steam iron and leave to cool. Place the fabric on a flat surface and lay the acetate circles from each trinket box and the glass circles from each frame on the fabric, spacing each piece fairly evenly. Carefully draw round the acetate and glass circles using the felt pen and remove the circles from the fabric.*

**3** *Cut out a square of fabric for each design, allowing at least 5cm (2in) of surplus fabric round each circular outline. Work a horizontal and vertical row of tacking stitches, using a different coloured thread, inside each drawn circle to mark the centre of the fabric. Mark the centre of each chart with a soft pencil.*

COLOUR / BACKSTITCH KEY: CELESTIAL GIFTS

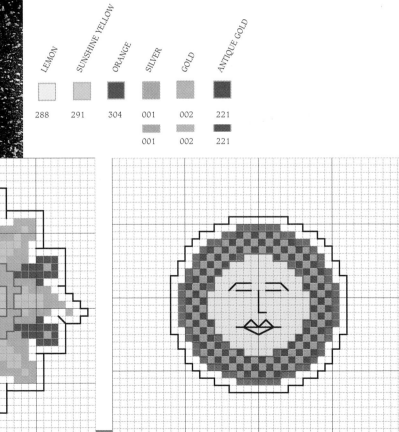

| LEMON | SUNSHINE YELLOW | ORANGE | SILVER | GOLD | ANTIQUE GOLD |
|---|---|---|---|---|---|
| 288 | 291 | 304 | 001 | 002 | 221 |
|  |  |  | 001 | 002 | 221 |

LARGE SUN

SMALL SUN

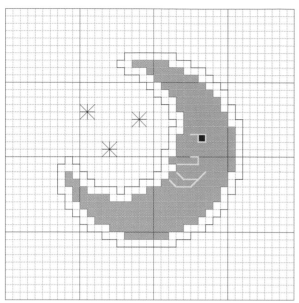

**MOON**

### WORKING THE STITCHES

Mount the fabric in the embroidery hoop (page 13). Work the designs from the charts, using the key as a guide. Work the cross stitch areas first, then add the remaining details. Instructions for cross stitch and the other embroidery stitches are given on pages 12-13. Work outwards from the centre of each design and use two strands of embroidery thread or one strand of metallic thread. Finally, work a French knot at the centre of each eye on the two sun designs using three strands of navy thread.

### MAKING UP THE GIFTS

**1** *Press the finished embroideries lightly on the wrong side. Press each piece over a padded surface and take care not to flatten the stitches.*

**2** *Cut out each embroidery along the circular outline and mount in the frames and box lids following the manufacturer's instructions.*

*Although perfect for trinket boxes you could use these motifs for decorating shirt collars, or a dark coloured tie.*

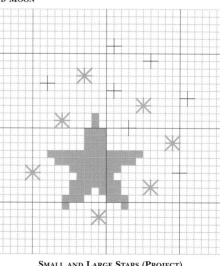

**SUN AND MOON**

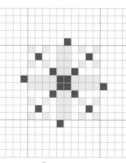

**SUNBURST**

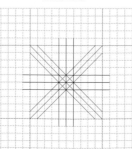

**BRIGHT STAR**

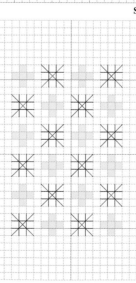

**SMALL STARS**

**SMALL AND LARGE STARS (PROJECT)**

**SMALL STARBURST (PROJECT)**

**GALAXY (PROJECT)**

**STARS**

# Birthday Cards

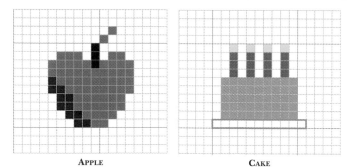

APPLE       CAKE       BOAT

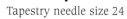

## WORKBASKET

❖

Small pieces of white 11 count
Aida large enough to
mount in a hoop

❖

DMC Stranded Cotton in the
following colours: white, black
310, dark grey 414, yellow 444,
crimson 666, grass green 703,
deep blue 798, mid blue 809,
pistachio 3348, pale clover 3689,
oak brown 3772, deep banana
3821 (this quantity of thread will
stitch several repeats
of the motifs)

❖

Tapestry needle size 24

❖

Embroidery hoop

❖

Tacking thread in a dark colour

❖

Sewing needle

❖

Ready-made greeting cards in
pastel colours and with a range of
aperture sizes

❖

Graph paper and coloured
pencils

❖

Narrow sticky tape and
double-sided sticky tape

## WORKING THE DESIGN

**1** *Choose one of the motifs from the
chart and sketch it out on graph
paper the required number of times,
leaving a gap of at least two squares*
between each motif. Draw a
rectangle around the outside of each
motif, and cut out along this line.

**2** *Using the photograph as a guide,
arrange the motifs on a piece of
graph paper, separating them by at
least one square. Add a number or
name to the design in the same way,
using the numbers on page 30 or
one of the alphabets from pages
68–69. When you are happy with
your arrangement, secure the motifs
with sticky tape.*

## WORKING THE STITCHES

Fold the fabric into four and
mark the centre with a few
tacking stitches. Mark the
centre of your chart with a soft
pencil. Mount the fabric in the
embroidery hoop (page 13).
  Work the design from the
chart in cross stitch (page 12)
using three strands of thread in
the needle throughout. Work
outwards from the centre,
remembering that each coloured
square on the chart represents
one complete cross stitch
worked over one woven block of
fabric.
  When all the cross stitch areas
have been completed, work the
linear details in back stitch
(page 12) from the chart. Use
three strands of thread in the
needle and work each stitch
over one fabric block.

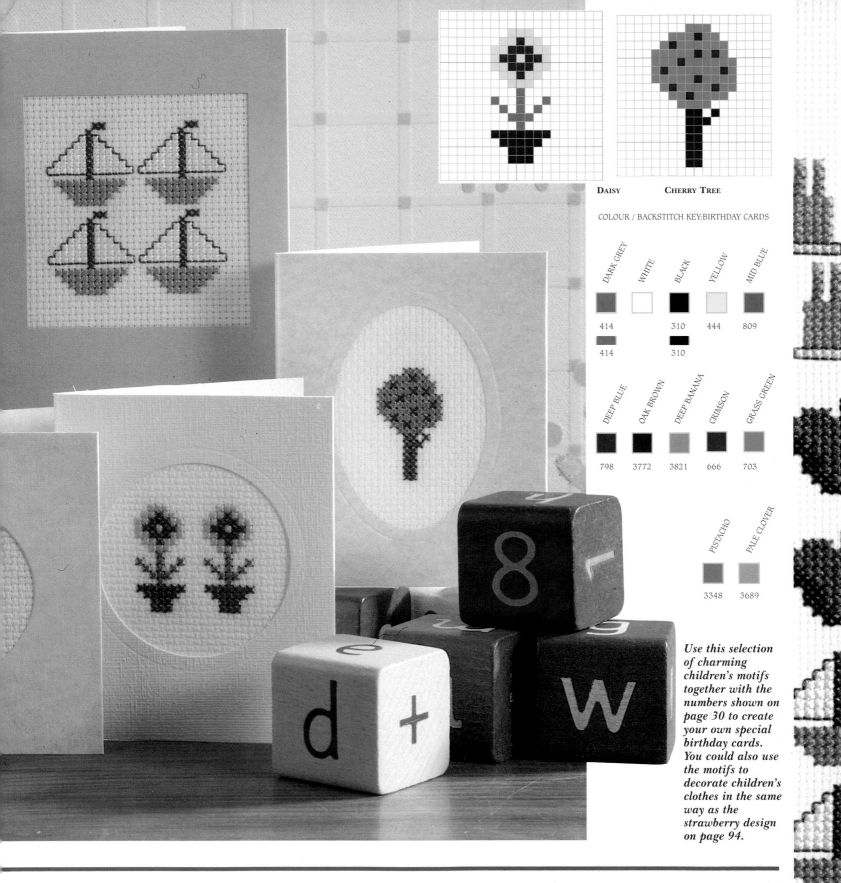

**DAISY**       **CHERRY TREE**

COLOUR / BACKSTITCH KEY: BIRTHDAY CARDS

| DARK GREY | WHITE | BLACK | YELLOW | MID BLUE |
|-----------|-------|-------|--------|----------|
| 414 | | 310 | 444 | 809 |
| 414 | | 310 | | |

| DEEP BLUE | OAK BROWN | DEEP BANANA | CRIMSON | GRASS GREEN |
|-----------|-----------|-------------|---------|-------------|
| 798 | 3772 | 3821 | 666 | 703 |

| PISTACHO | PALE CLOVER |
|----------|-------------|
| 3348 | 3689 |

*Use this selection of charming children's motifs together with the numbers shown on page 30 to create your own special birthday cards. You could also use the motifs to decorate children's clothes in the same way as the strawberry design on page 94.*

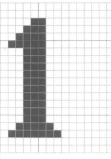
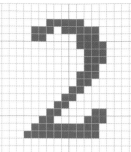
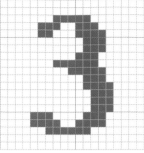
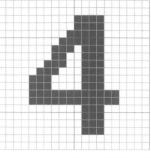
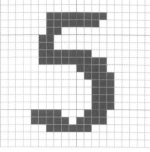

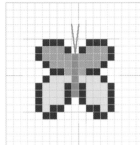

**BUTTERFLY**

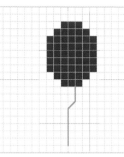

**RED BALLOON**

*Smaller motifs are perfect for cards, and you could adapt other designs. The fish motifs on page 42 would also make good designs for cards.*

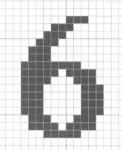

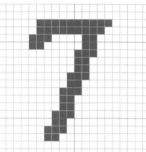

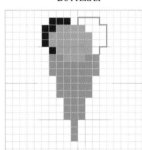

**ICE CREAM**

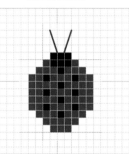

**LADYBIRD**

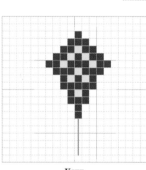

**KITE**

*Alphabets and numbers are always useful when working and designing with cross stitch. Small alphabets are also good for personalising pieces of work.*

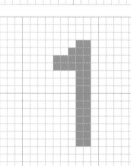

## MAKING UP THE CARDS

**1** *Choose a card with an aperture which accommodates your embroidery comfortably. Most craft stores offer a wide range of cards with different apertures.*

**2** *Stick narrow strips of double-sided tape round the aperture on the wrong side of the card. Carefully peel off the backing paper on the tape.*

**3** *Lay the embroidery on a flat surface with right side facing and place the taped side of the card over the top, ensuring the design is central.*

**4** *Press firmly to secure, then carefully trim away the surplus fabric round the aperture. Stick the flap over the wrong side of the trimmed embroidery, again using double-sided tape.*

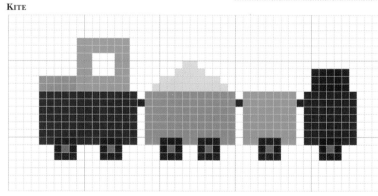

**TRAIN**

ABCDEFGHIJKLMNOPQRSTU

ABCDEFGHIJKLMNOPQRSTUVW

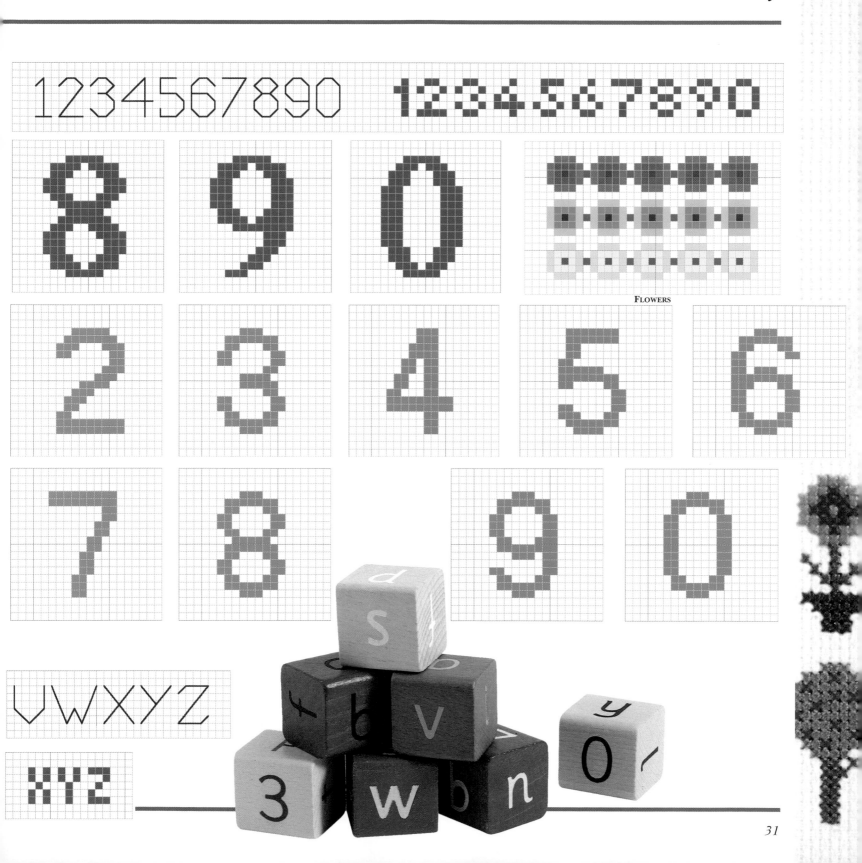

1234567890

1234567890

8 9 0

**FLOWERS**

2 3 4 5 6

7 8 9 0

UWXYZ

XYZ

3 w n

# Wedding Keepsakes

## WORKBASKET

❖

1 skein of DMC Stranded Cotton in each of the following colours: deep lavender 333, mid lavender 340, pale lavender 341, mid pink 604, pale pink 948, grey green 3816

❖

Tapestry needle size 26

❖

Tacking cotton in a dark colour and sewing needle

❖

Embroidery hoop or rectangular frame

❖

### For the sampler

30 x 25cm (12 x 10in) of white 14 count Aida (you will need a larger piece to accommodate longer names)

❖

Wooden picture frame with aperture 17.5 x 16cm (7 x 6½in) (you will need a larger frame to accommodate longer names)

❖

Stiff white card and backing board to fit picture frame

❖

Crochet cotton or very fine string

❖

Large needle with big eye

❖

Glass-headed dressmaking pins

❖

Gummed paper strip and graph paper and pencil

❖

### For the ring pillow

20 x 20cm (8 x 8in) of white 14 count Aida fabric

❖

20 x 20cm (8 x 8in) white felt

❖

Three pieces wadding 11 x 11cm (4½ x 4½in)

❖

50cm (20in) narrow pink satin ribbon and 60cm (24in) flat or ruffled white lace edging

❖

Matching sewing thread and pins

## PREPARING THE SAMPLER

**1** *Using the alphabet on pages 68–69, sketch out the names and date for the sampler on a strip of graph paper, leaving one square between each letter and number.*

**2** *Arrange the names in the same way as Anna and Max are shown on the original chart unless the names you have chosen are longer than four letters each. In that case, arrange the names beneath each other, separated by the back stitch scroll and positioned two squares apart.*

**3** *If you position the names beneath each other you will also need to make the sampler deeper. Do this by working one extra border motif down each side.*

**RING PILLOW**

COLOUR / BACKSTITCH KEY:
WEDDING KEEPSAKES

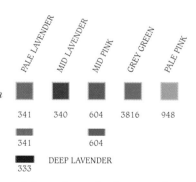

| PALE LAVENDER | MID LAVENDER | MID PINK | GREY GREEN | PALE PINK |
|---|---|---|---|---|
| 341 | 340 | 604 | 3816 | 948 |
| 341 | | 604 | | |
| DEEP LAVENDER 333 | | | | |

*A framed sampler bearing the bride's and groom's names and their wedding date decorated with a heart and a border of flowers make the perfect wedding gift. Complement the sampler with a lace-trimmed ring pillow.*

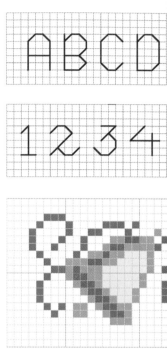

**LOVE HEART**

*If you wish to make the sampler larger you can repeat the heart design below the names.*

### WORKING THE SAMPLER

Fold the fabric to find the centre and mark with tacking stitches. Mark the chart centre with a soft pencil. Mount the fabric (page 13). Work the design in cross stitch (page 12) and back stitch (page 12) from the chart using three strands of thread. Each square on the chart represents one complete cross stitch worked over one woven fabric block.

### MAKING UP

*1 Press the embroidery with a warm iron on the wrong side over a well-padded surface. Allow the fabric to cool.*

*2 Position the embroidery centrally over the card, with the wrong side facing the card. Fold over the top of the fabric and check the position of the embroidery with the window mount. Secure the fold with pins pushed right into the edge of the card. Repeat along the bottom edge, taking care to keep the fabric grain straight.*

*3 Using a long piece of crochet cotton and the large needle, take long stitches between the two fabric edges, starting at the top left. When you have reached the other side, remove the pins. Knot the thread at the starting point, then pull the thread downwards, tightening it as you work. Tightly secure the thread ends.*

*4 Repeat the pinning and lacing along the remaining two sides of the fabric, folding in the corners neatly. Place the glass, window mount, laced picture and backing board in the frame and fix the layers in place with tacks. Seal the gap between the backing board and the frame using gummed paper strip.*

### WORKING THE PILLOW

Fold the fabric in four to find the centre and mark with a few tacking stitches. Mark the centre of your chart with a soft pencil. Mount the fabric in the hoop (page 13).

Work the design in cross stitch (page 12) and back stitch (page 12) from the chart using three strands of thread in the tapestry needle. Work outwards from the centre of the design, remembering that each coloured square on the chart represents one complete cross stitch worked over one woven fabric block.

### MAKING UP THE PILLOW

*1 Press the embroidery lightly with a warm iron on the wrong side over a well-padded surface, taking care not to crush the stitches. Trim away the surplus fabric round the embroidery, leaving a margin of twelve unworked fabric blocks all round the edge.*

*2 Leaving six unworked fabric blocks showing all round the edge*

# F G H I J K L M N O P Q R S T U V W X Y Z

# 5 6 7 8 9 0

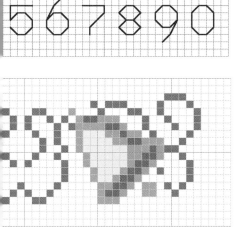

**BELL BORDER**

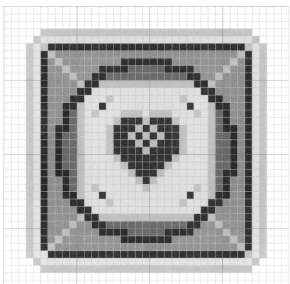

**FLOWER HEART**

*These more intricate heart designs could be used on a ring pillow or to add a different look to the sampler.*

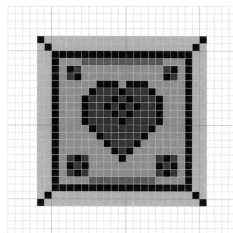

**HEARTS**

turn under the raw edge and tack in place. On the wrong side, tack the lace edging in position close to the folded edge of the fabric, easing the corners so they lie flat.

**3** Place the embroidery on a flat surface with the wrong side facing and cover with the three pieces of wadding – you may need to trim the wadding as each piece should be slightly smaller than the embroidery. Place the white felt centrally on top of the wadding and pin all the layers in place. Turn over and tack the layers together close to the edge of the fabric.

**4** Machine stitch round the edge with matching thread, positioning the row of stitches two blocks from the edge of the fabric. Remove all the tacking stitches and, holding the lace edging out of the way, carefully trim away the felt close to the machine stitching. Finally, fold the ribbon in half and attach securely to the centre of the pillow.

# Novel Books

### WORKBASKET

❖

Two pieces of cream perforated paper 12.5 x 20.5cm (5 x 8in) for the address books

❖

Two strips of cream perforated paper about 5cm (2in) wide for the bookmarks

❖

DMC Stranded Cotton in the following colours: 2 skeins of tan 3826; 1 skein of soft grey 452, grey green 3817, pale walnut 3828 (this quantity of thread will stitch inserts for two books, plus bookmarks)

❖

Tapestry needle size 24

❖

Two address and birthday books from Framecraft (page 108)

❖

Soft pencil

*Embroider inserts for two address and birthday books, complete with matching bookmarks, on cream perforated paper using autumnal shades of green, soft grey and brown. Keep one of the books for yourself and give the other as a gift to a special friend.*

BIRTHDAY BOOK & BOOKMARK

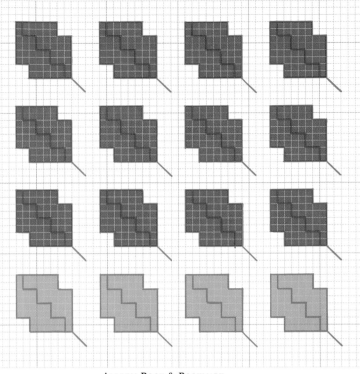

COLOUR / BACKSTITCH KEY:
NOVEL BOOKS

PALE WALNUT · GREY GREEN · SOFT GREY

3828    3817    452

### PREPARING THE PAPER

**1** *Slide out the inserts and sheets of acetate from the books. Carefully slide a piece of perforated paper behind each oval aperture. Mark the aperture shape on to the paper with the pencil, pressing very lightly.*

**2** *Slide out the paper and mark the centre of the drawn oval with the pencil. Mark the centre of the chart in the same way.*

### WORKING THE STITCHES

Working outwards from the centre, stitch the leaf designs in cross stitch (page 12) from the charts using four strands of thread in the needle. Each coloured square on the chart represents one complete cross stitch worked over two vertical and two horizontal 'threads' of paper.

When all the cross stitch areas have been completed, work the linear details in back stitch (page 12) from the chart using three strands of thread. Work each back stitch over one 'thread' of paper.

### MAKING UP THE BOOKS

**1** *Lay one piece of acetate over a piece of embroidered paper and carefully slide both layers into the address book. Repeat the process for the second book.*

### MAKING UP BOOKMARKS

**1** *Using the photograph as a guide, work a section of the design at the top of each strip of paper. Work a single row of backstitch round the strip, two 'threads' from the edge, leaving the top two corners straight or working several stitches at an angle and trimming away the surplus paper diagonally.*

# Stylish living

Add a touch of class to your home with cross stitch.
Make a pretty shelf edging worked in shades of blue
and white for the kitchen, lacy cushions for the bedroom
or living room, and even decorations for the
Christmas tree.

# On The Edge

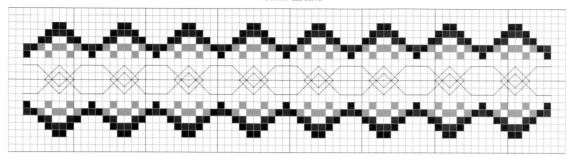

## WORKBASKET

❖

White 11 count Aida
DMC Stranded Cotton in the
following colours: dark blue 797,
mid blue 799, pale blue 800

❖

Tapestry needle size 24

❖

Embroidery hoop

❖

Tacking thread in a dark colour

❖

Matching sewing thread

❖

Sewing needle and pins

❖

Length of narrow lace edging to
trim each worked band, one
length per band

❖

Self-adhesive fixing pads or
double-sided sticky tape for fixing
the edging on to the shelves

## MEASURING UP

Measure the length of the
shelves and add 1.5cm (¹/₂in) to
each end for turnings.

The embroidery is worked in
a band on a strip of fabric, then
the raw edges are turned under.
The finished edging is 4.5cm
(1³/₄in) deep, so each strip needs
to be at least 7.5cm (3in) deep to
allow for turnings.

To calculate the amount of
lace edging you need to buy,
multiply the length
measurement plus turnings by
the number of shelves you
intend to edge.

## PREPARING THE FABRIC

**1** *Mark the size of the shelf edging
on the fabric with rows of tacking,
positioning the strips side-by-side
and remembering to allow for
turnings.*

**2** *Mark the centre of each strip both
lengthways and widthways with rows
of tacking. Mount the centre of the
fabric in the hoop (page 13).*

## WORKING THE STITCHES

Work the repeating border from
the chart in cross stitch (page
12) and back stitch (page 12)
starting at the centre of each
strip and working
out. Use three strands of thread
in the needle, and remember
that each square on the chart
represents one cross stitch
worked over one block of fabric.

## MAKING UP THE EDGING

**1** *Press the embroidery lightly on the
wrong side with a warm iron. Cut
out the embroidered strips along the
tacked lines. Turn under 1.5cm
(¹/₂in) along the edge, leaving two
unworked blocks showing along the
top and bottom of the embroidery.*

**2** *Pin and tack in position. Work a
row of stitching round the edge of
each strip, one block from the fold.*

**3** *Slipstitch the lace along the lower
edge of each piece. Press the strips
lightly, and fix in position.*

COLOUR / BACKSTITCH KEY: SHELF EDGING

| PALE BLUE | MID BLUE | DARK BLUE |
|---|---|---|
| | | |
| 800 | 799 | 797 |

799

*Stitched in three shades of blue,
the geometric design is quick to
work and perfectly set off with a
narrow lace edging.*

*The designs given below could be
used in conjunction with the
main chart to give a different
edge design for each shelf.*

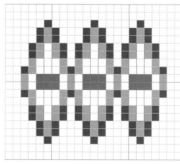

**BUSY BORDERS**

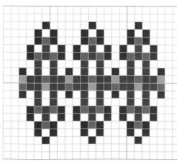

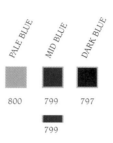

# Tropical Towels

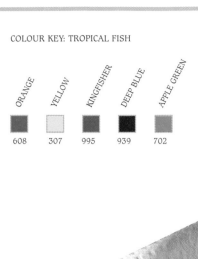

## WORKBASKET

❖

White 11 count Aida

❖

DMC Stranded Cotton in
the following colours: yellow 307,
orange 608, apple
green 702, deep blue 939,
kingfisher 995

❖

Tapestry needle size 24

❖

Embroidery hoop

❖

Tacking thread in a dark colour

❖

Sewing needle

❖

White guest towels and facecloth
with a woven band

❖

Fusible bonding web

### PREPARING THE FABRIC

**1** *Measure the woven strip across
your towels and add 1.5cm (¹/₂in) all
round. Mark the finished size of the
bands on the fabric with rows of
tacking, positioning the bands
side-by-side.*

**2** *Find the centre of each band and
mark with a few stitches.*

### COLOUR KEY: TROPICAL FISH

| ORANGE | YELLOW | KINGFISHER | DEEP BLUE | APPLE GREEN |
|--------|--------|------------|-----------|-------------|
| 608 | 307 | 995 | 939 | 702 |

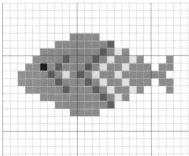

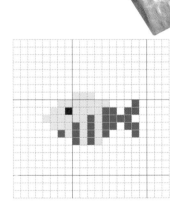

**FISH MOTIFS**

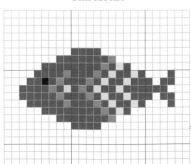

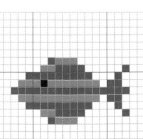

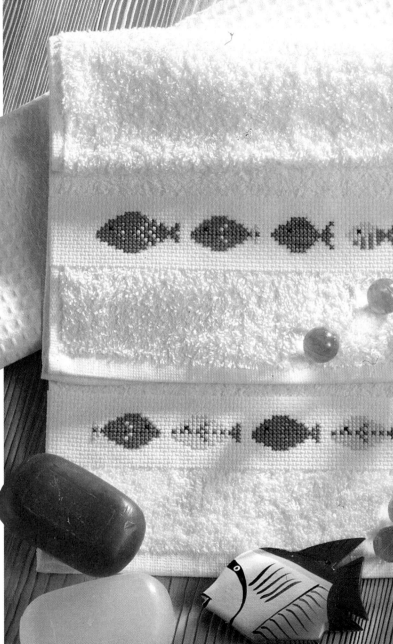

## WORKING THE STITCHES

Mount the centre of the fabric in the hoop or frame (page 13).

Work the fish design in cross stitch (page 12) from the chart using three strands of thread in the tapestry needle throughout.

Work outwards from the centre of the design, remembering that each coloured square on the chart represents one complete cross stitch worked over one woven block of fabric.

For the facecloth decoration, work one motif in cross stitch on a small piece of Aida.

## MAKING UP THE TOWELS

**1** *Press the embroidery lightly with a warm iron on the wrong side over a well-padded surface, taking care not to crush the stitches. Following the manufacturer's instructions, carefully iron a piece of fusible bonding web on to the back of the embroidery.*

**2** *When the pieces are cool, cut out the bands along the tacked lines. Apply bonding web to the facecloth motif in the same way and cut the fabric into rectangle.*

**3** *Peel away the backing paper from the bands and position each one over the woven band on the towels, folding over 1.5cm (¹/₂in) at each end on to the wrong side of the towel.*

**4** *Press the bands with a steam iron (or an ordinary iron and a damp cloth) to attach them. Repeat with the single motif, positioning it in one corner of the facecloth.*

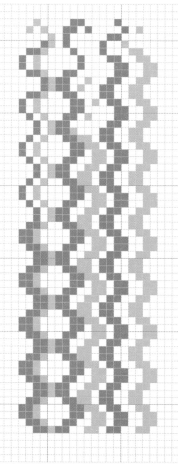

**SEAWEED**

*Tropical fish decorate guest towels and a facecloth, adding a touch of Caribbean sunshine to your bathroom. The embroidered bands and single motifs are applied with fusible bonding web.*

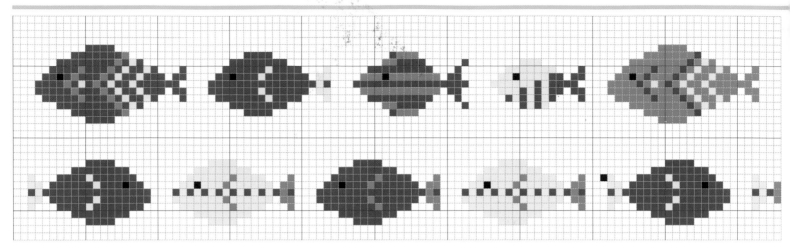

**FISHY FRIEZE**

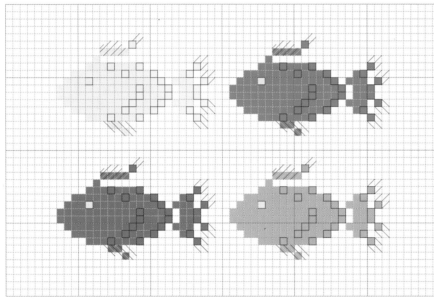

**MINNOWS**

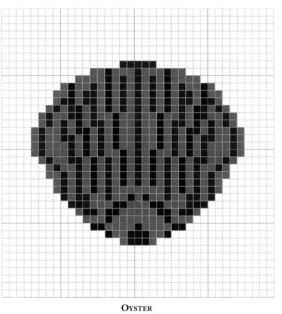

**OYSTER**

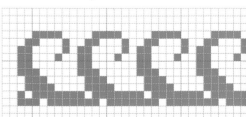

**WONDERFUL WAVES**

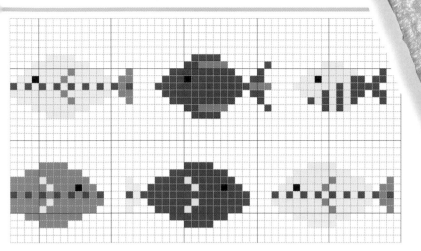

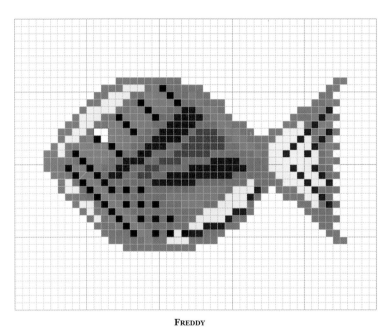

**FREDDY**

Fish are good motifs to use on towels, and you could add a seaweed border below your fish design if you want to ring the changes. Alternative fish motifs, a shell and a larger fish are given which could be used on flannels or face towels, or in place of the other fish designs.

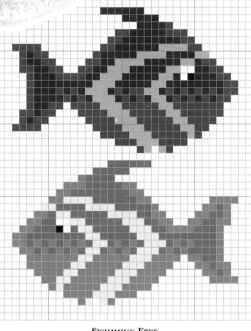

**SWIMMING FREE**

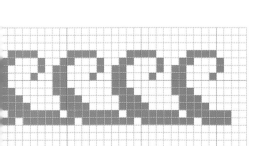

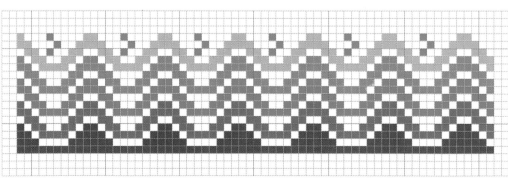

**CAT CLOCK**

COLOUR / BACKSTITCH KEY: PERFECT TIME

| TAN | GRASS GREEN | YELLOW | ORANGE |
|-----|-------------|--------|--------|
| 3826 | 703 | 307 | 740 |

703

| | DARK GREY | | DARK GREEN |
|---|---|---|---|
| 413 | | 3808 | |

*Four ginger cats stand guard over groups of flowers to make a pretty decoration on this clock face. You may like to use a different colour combination to reflect cats you know personally, perhaps stitching one black, one white, one tortoiseshell and one tabby cat.*

## WORKBASKET

✤

10 x 15cm (4 x 6in) cream perforated paper

✤

1 skein of DMC Stranded Cotton in each of the following colours: yellow 307, dark grey 413, grass green 703, orange 740, dark green 3808, tan 3826

✤

Tapestry needle size 24

✤

Small wooden clock from Framecraft (page 108)

✤

Soft pencil

## PREPARING THE PAPER

**1** Mark out a rectangular area on the paper 48 'threads' wide and 72 'threads' deep with the pencil. These lines are your cutting lines.

**2** Mark the centre of the paper with the pencil, and also mark the centre of the chart in the same way.

**3** The lines at the centre of the chart indicate the portion which will be cut away to accommodate the clock spindle. Mark these lines on the paper.

## WORKING THE STITCHES

Working outwards from the centre, stitch the design in cross stitch (page 12) from the chart using three strands of thread in the needle.

Each coloured square on the chart represents one complete cross stitch worked over one 'thread' of paper.

When all the cross stitch areas have been completed, work the linear details and numerals in back stitch (page 12) from the chart using three strands of thread.

Work each back stitch over one 'thread' of perforated paper.

## FINISHING THE CLOCK

**1** Following the manufacturer's instructions, take the clock to pieces. Cut away the central portion of paper, and also trim the edges, following the cutting lines.

**2** Position the paper carefully in the clock, matching the central holes. Carefully, reassemble the clock following the instructions.

*Why not make a picture to co-ordinate with the clock face? You could add in some different motifs, like the ones here.*

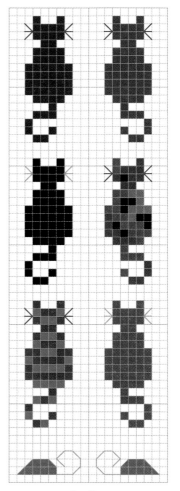

**SLY CATS**

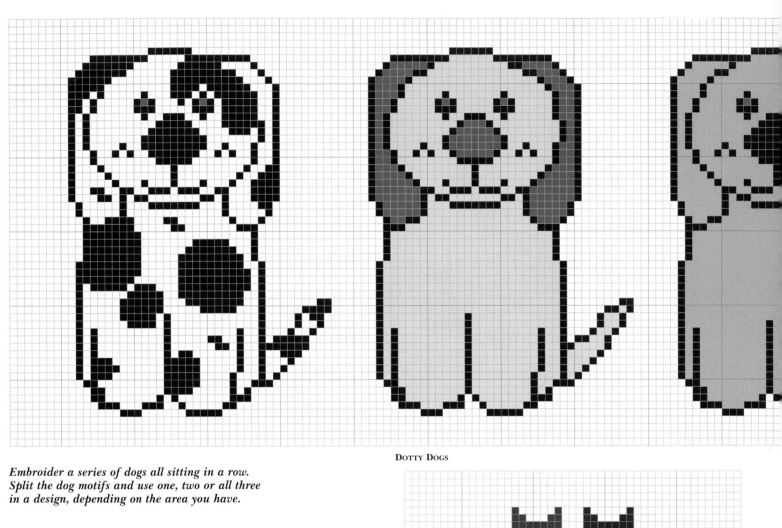

**DOTTY DOGS**

*Embroider a series of dogs all sitting in a row.
Split the dog motifs and use one, two or all three
in a design, depending on the area you have.*

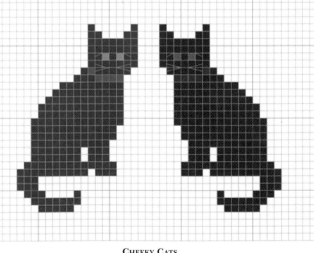

**CHEEKY CATS**

**MINI MICE**

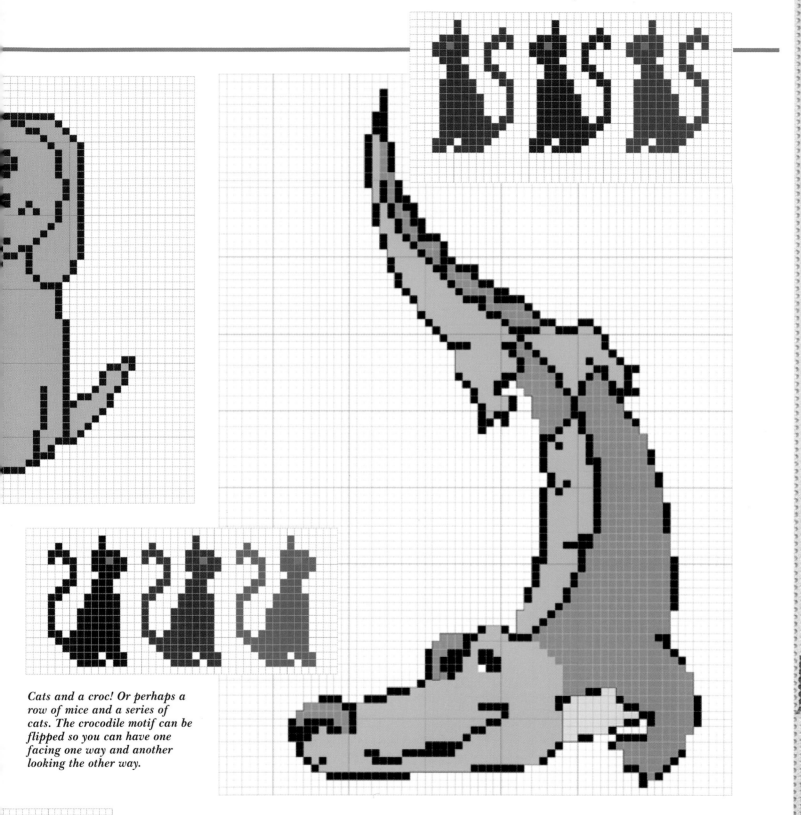

Cats and a croc! Or perhaps a row of mice and a series of cats. The crocodile motif can be flipped so you can have one facing one way and another looking the other way.

# Lacy Cushions

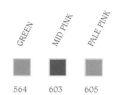

## WORKBASKET

❖

8 x 8cm (3¹/₄ x 3¹/₄in) pieces of
8 mesh waste canvas, one for
each motif

❖

DMC Stranded Cotton in the
following colours: mid pink 603,
pale pink 605, green 564 (1 skein
of each colour will work about
twelve sprigs)

❖

Crewel needle size 7

❖

Tacking thread in a dark colour

❖

Sewing needle and pins

❖

Two white lacy cushion covers
(Either buy ready-made covers or
make you own, if you require a
special size)

❖

Two cushion pads to fit the
covers

## PREPARING THE COVERS

**1** *Pin three or four squares of waste
canvas at random on the front of
each cushion cover.*

**2** *When you are happy with the
arrangement, tack each square
securely to the cover and mark the
centre of the squares with a few
tacking stitches.*

**3** *Mark the centre of the chart with a
soft pencil.*

## WORKING THE STITCHES

Work the embroidery from the
chart in cross stitch (page 12)
using three strands of thread in
the crewel needle throughout.
   Work outwards from the
centre of the design
remembering that each coloured
square on the chart represents
one complete cross stitch
worked over one vertical
and one horizontal double
thread of canvas.

COLOUR KEY: LACY CUSHIONS

GREEN    MID PINK   PALE PINK

564      603        605

## FINISHING THE COVERS

**1** *Press the embroidery lightly on the
wrong side over a well-padded
surface to set the stitches.*

**2** *Wet the canvas, and remove the
canvas threads using tweezers.*

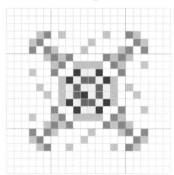

**SIMPLE SPRIGS**

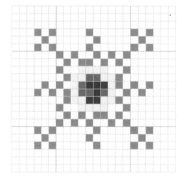

*Strew tiny pink and green flower
sprigs across a pair of
ready-made white lacy cushion
covers. The embroidery is quick
and easy to work using the waste
canvas method described on page
13. Ring the changes by adding
in alternative designs, from the
selection given above.*

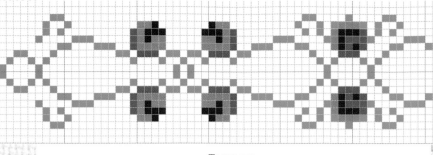

# Delicate Traycloth

### WORKBASKET

❖

54 x 37cm (21½ x 14¾in) of ivory
18 count Aida

❖

1 skein of DMC Stranded
Cotton in each of the
following colours: mid
peach 352, grass green 704,
deep peach 3712,
pale peach 3779

❖

Tapestry needle size 26

❖

Crewel needle size 8

❖

Embroidery hoop

❖

Tacking thread in a dark colour

❖

Sewing needle and pins

### PREPARING THE FABRIC

**1** *Work a row of tacking stitches
across one short end of the fabric
6cm (2½in) from the raw edge.
Working towards the opposite end of
the fabric, work a second row of
tacking 32 blocks from the first,
forming a band. The band marks the
position of the embroidery.*

**2** *Fold the fabric in half to find the
centre of the band and mark with a
row of tacking. Mark the centre of
the chart with a soft pencil.*

### WORKING THE STITCHES

Mount the centre of the band in
an embroidery hoop (page 13).
Work the flower pattern from
the chart in cross stitch (page

COLOUR KEY: TRAYCLOTH

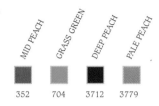

MID PEACH 352 · GRASS GREEN 704 · DEEP PEACH 3712 · PALE PEACH 3779

12) starting at the centre of the
tacked band and working
outwards.

Use three strands of thread in
the tapestry needle
throughout and remember that
each coloured square on the
chart represents one complete
cross stitch worked over two
vertical and two horizontal
blocks of fabric.

### FINISHING OFF

**1** *Press the embroidery lightly on the
wrong side over a well-padded
surface. Use a warm iron and take
care not to crush the delicate
stitching.*

**2** *Pin and tack a 1cm (½in) double
hem round the traycloth, turning in
the corners neatly and making sure
that the hemline falls between two
rows of fabric blocks.*

**3** *Secure the hem with a row of
running stitches or back stitch (page
12). Work each stitch over two
fabric blocks. Use two strands of pale
peach embroidery cotton in the crewel
needle and position the stitches five
blocks from the hemline fold.*

A band of floral motifs linked by twining stems is embroidered in shades of peach and green to decorate a delicate, ivory-coloured traycloth. Work the band at one or both ends of the traycloth and finish off the hem with a row of running stitches worked in pale peach thread.

ROSE HIGHLIGHT

If you have a favourite set of china you could alter the colours to co-ordinate. Strawberries (see page 94) or other fruit make good designs for traycloths.

53

# Art Deco Settings

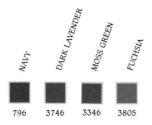

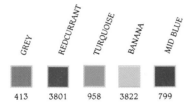

### WORKBASKET

❖

39 x 32cm (15¹/₂ x 13in) of antique white 11 count Aida for the placemat

❖

39 x 39cm (15¹/₂ x 15¹/₂in) of antique white 11 count Aida for the napkin

❖

1 skein of DMC Stranded Cotton in each of the following colours: grey 413, navy 796, mid blue 799, turquoise 958, moss green 3346, dark lavender 3746, redcurrant 3801, fuchsia 3805, banana 3822

❖

Tapestry needle size 24

❖

Crewel needle size 7

❖

Embroidery hoop

❖

Tacking thread in a dark colour

❖

Sewing needle and pins

COLOUR KEY: ART DECO SETTINGS

| GREY | REDCURRANT | TURQUOISE | BANANA | MID BLUE |
|------|-----------|-----------|--------|----------|
| 413 | 3801 | 958 | 3822 | 799 |

| NAVY | DARK LAVENDER | MOSS GREEN | FUCHSIA |
|------|---------------|------------|---------|
| 796 | 3746 | 3346 | 3805 |

*Make a placemat special by decorating it with a coloured band of Art Deco patterns. Co-ordinate a napkin by repeating a section of the chart.*

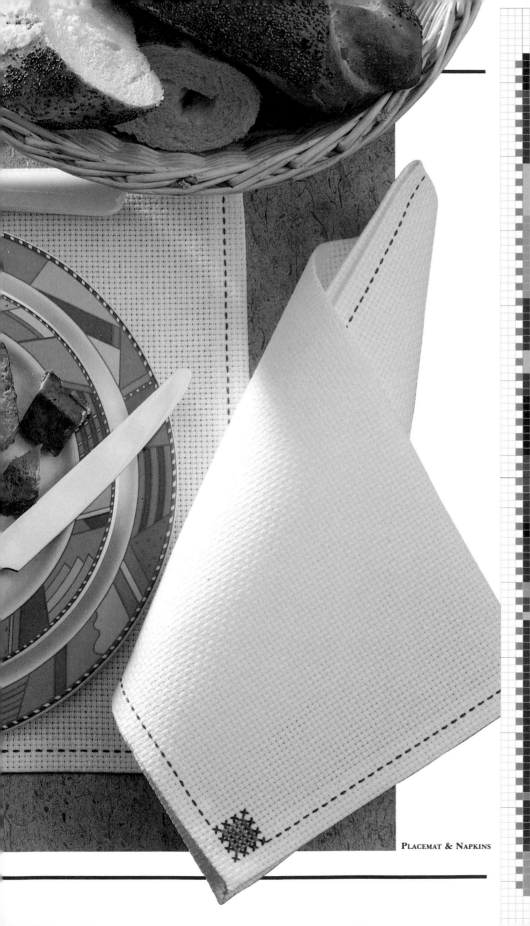

PLACEMAT & NAPKINS

### PREPARING THE FABRIC

**1** *Work a row of tacking stitches across one short end of the fabric 5.5cm (2¹/₄in) from the raw edge. Working towards the opposite end of the fabric, work a second row of tacking seven blocks from the first, forming a band. The band marks the position of the embroidery.*

**2** *Fold the fabric in half to find the centre of the band and mark with a row of tacking. Mark the centre of the chart with a soft pencil.*

### WORKING THE PLACEMAT

Mount the centre of the band in the hoop (page 13). Work the geometric pattern from the chart in cross stitch (page 12) starting at the centre and working out. Use three strands of thread in the needle and remember that each coloured square on the chart represents one complete cross stitch worked over one block of fabric.

### MAKING UP

**1** *Press the embroidery lightly on the wrong side. Use a warm iron and take care not to crush the stitching.*

**2** *Pin and tack a 1.5cm (¹/₂in) double hem round the traycloth, turning in the corners neatly and making sure that the hemline falls between two rows of fabric blocks. Secure the hem with a row of back stitch (page 12). Work each stitch over one fabric block using three strands of thread in the needle.*

### WORKING THE NAPKIN

**1** *Finish the edge of the napkin following step 2 above.*

**2** *Using the photograph as a guide, work a small section to form a seven block square and complete the corner. Press the with a warm iron.*

# Tabletop Tulips

## WORKBASKET

✣

130 x 130cm (52 x 52in) of white
18 count Damask Aida for the
cloth, plus six 45 x 45cm (18 x
18in) pieces for the napkins

✣

DMC Stranded Cotton in the
following colours:
4 skeins of kingfisher 996;
3 skeins of dark blue 798,
golden yellow 972;
2 skeins of apple green 703,
grass green 912, light
yellow 973, yellow green
3348, mid blue 3755

✣

Tapestry needle size 24

✣

Small and large
embroidery hoops

✣

Tacking thread in a dark colour

✣

Matching sewing thread

✣

Sewing needle and pins

## PREPARING THE CLOTH

**1** *Tack a line 7cm (3in) from the
edge of the fabric to mark the inner
edge of the hem, then a second line
6.5cm (2³/₄in) inside the first line.
The second line marks the base of
each large tulip motif.*

**2** *Using the close-up photograph as
a guide, tack rectangular shapes to
mark the position of the eight tulip
motifs round the tablecloth,
arranging two motifs in each
corner. Ensure that each rectangle
is 78 by 114 fabric blocks in size
and make sure that the base of each
tulip motif falls along the inner
tacked line.*

**3** *Tack a third line round the cloth,
this time taking the stitches through
the exact centre of each tacked
rectangle. This line will help you to
position the running stitch border
after all the tulip motifs have
been worked.*

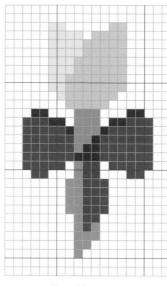

**TULIP NAPKIN**

COLOUR / RUNNING STITCH KEY: TULIPS

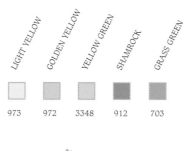

| LIGHT YELLOW | GOLDEN YELLOW | YELLOW GREEN | SHAMROCK | GRASS GREEN |
|---|---|---|---|---|
| 973 | 972 | 3348 | 912 | 703 |

| DARK BLUE | KINGFISHER | MID BLUE |
|---|---|---|
| 798 | 996 | 3755 |
| 798 | | 3755 |

*Welcome the warmer days of
spring by setting your table with
this delightful cloth and set of
napkins featuring stylised
bunches of tulips. Both the cloth
and the napkins are the perfect
size for a light afternoon tea of
scones with home-made preserves
and thick cream or thinly cut
sandwiches.*

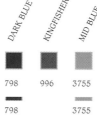

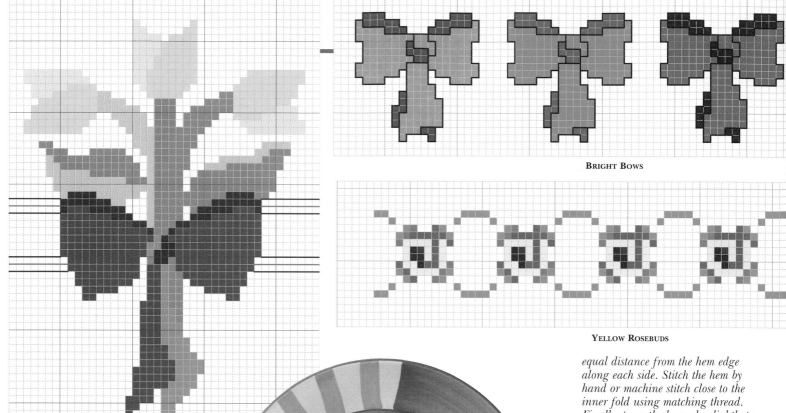

**BRIGHT BOWS**

**YELLOW ROSEBUDS**

**TULIP TABLECLOTH**

## WORKING THE CLOTH

Mount the evenweave fabric in the large embroidery hoop (page 13) and work each tulip motif in cross stitch (page 12) from the large chart, using three strands of embroidery thread in the needle throughout.

Note that each coloured square given on the chart represents one complete cross stitch worked over two vertical and two horizontal fabric blocks.

When all the motifs have been completed, work lines of running stitches or back stitches (page 12) to link the tulip motifs together.

The position and colour of each line is represented as a solid line on the chart. Use three strands of mid blue or three strands of dark blue thread and work each stitch over two blocks of fabric.

## MAKING UP THE CLOTH

*1 Press the embroidery lightly on the wrong side over a padded surface.*

*2 Work with a cool iron, taking care not to press too hard and crush the delicate stitching.*

*3 Pin and tack a hem round the cloth, making sure that the hemline fold runs neatly between two fabric blocks and that the embroidery is an* equal distance from the hem edge along each side. Stitch the hem by hand or machine stitch close to the inner fold using matching thread. Finally, press the hem edge lightly to make a crisp fold.

## PREPARING THE NAPKINS

*1 Work a line of tacking stitches 2cm (³/₄in) from the edge of each napkin to mark the inner edge of the hem.*

*2 Mark the position of one small tulip motif on each napkin with a rectangle of tacking stitches measuring 30 by 54 fabric blocks.*

*3 Position the motif in one corner, about 6cm (2¹/₂in) from the tacked lines on two adjacent sides of the napkin.*

## WORKING THE NAPKINS

Mount the corner of the fabric in the small embroidery hoop (page 13) and work the small tulip motif from the chart in cross stitch (page 12) using three strands of embroidery thread in the needle throughout.

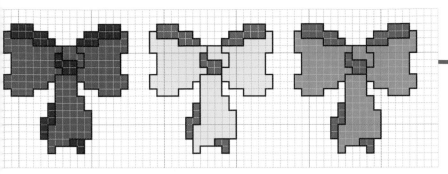

*Brightly coloured bows make an interesting motif for a tablecloth. Add interest by working a border between the motifs, using one of the designs here, rather than a simple row of backstich.*

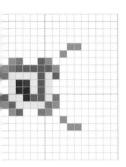

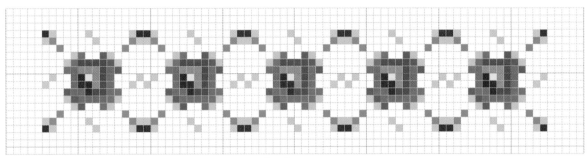

**RED ROSEBUDS**

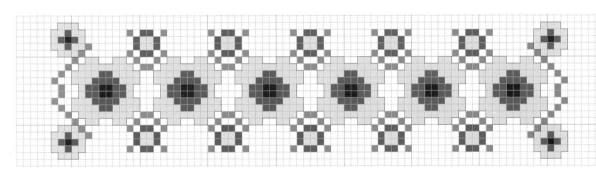

**PRETTY PANSIES**

*Floral motifs always work well on tablecloths, napkins, traycloths and even tablerunners. Alternatively, use them on hankies, or even neck scarves.*

Each coloured square on the chart represents one complete cross stitch worked over two vertical and two horizontal fabric blocks.

### MAKING UP THE NAPKINS

**1** *Press the embroidery lightly on the wrong side, then pin and tack a narrow double hem round the edge, turning in the corners neatly.*

**2** *Secure the hem with hand or machine stitching using a matching sewing thread.*

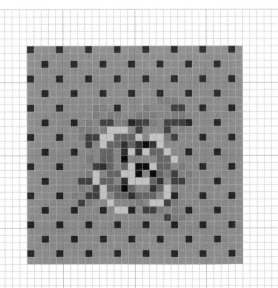

**PINK ROSE**

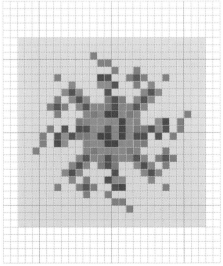

**FLOWER SPRAY**

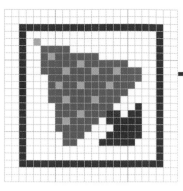

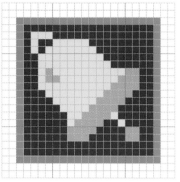

**CHRISTMAS CARDS & TREE DECORATION**

### WORKBASKET

❖

#### For the cards

5 x 5cm (2 x 2in) of white perforated paper for each card

❖

1 skein of DMC Stranded Cotton in each of the following colours: white, scarlet 666, pine green 699, grass green 702, yellow 973, brown 3031

❖

Tapestry needle size 24 and Crewel needle size 9

❖

9 x 18cm (3¹/₂ x 7in) gold card and 1 pack gold 00557 Mill Hill glass seed beads

❖

Double-sided sticky tape

❖

#### For the tree decorations

Two 20 thread x 20 thread pieces of 10 mesh plastic canvas for each decoration

❖

1 skein of DMC Tapestry Wool in each of the following colours: white, scarlet 7666, pine green 7906, grass green 7915, yellow 7786, brown 7467 (you will need 1 extra skein of pine green to work each plain back piece)

# Christmas Treats

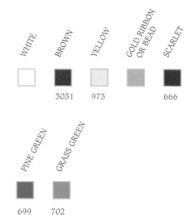

❖
1 spool DMC metallic embroidery ribbon in dark gold 276
❖
Tapestry needle size 22
❖
50cm (20in) narrow gold ribbon and one gold-coloured jump ring for each decoration
❖
Fine-point black felt pen with permanent ink

**COLOUR KEY: CHRISTMAS**

| WHITE | BROWN | YELLOW | GOLD RIBBON OR BEAD | SCARLET |
|---|---|---|---|---|
|  | 3031 | 973 |  | 666 |

| PINE GREEN | GRASS GREEN |
|---|---|
| 699 | 702 |

## WORKING THE CARDS

Mark the centre of each paper square with a pencil and mark the chart centre similarly.

Work the designs in cross stitch (page 12) omitting the gold stitches. Work out from the centre, using three strands of thread in the needle and remember that each square on the charts represents one cross stitch worked over one vertical and one horizontal 'thread'.

Work the gold squares in cross stitch using two strands of yellow in the crewel needle and attaching one gold bead with the top diagonal of every stitch.

## MAKING UP THE CARDS

*1 Score each rectangle of gold card across the width to make a 9 x 9cm (3¹/₂ x 3¹/₂in) folded card. Trim away the surplus paper from round the embroidery, leaving a margin of three unworked paper 'threads'.*

*2 Stick strips of double-sided tape on the back of the embroidered squares. Peel off the backing paper and stitch each square centrally on the gold card, making sure that the fold is at the left of the card.*

**Give a new lease of life to four traditional Christmas motifs – cross stitch the designs on perforated paper and make cards, or work them in wool on canvas to decorate your tree.**

## WORKING TREE TREATS

Carefully trim off any tiny bumps of plastic round each piece so that the outer edge is perfectly smooth.

To make the decoration fronts, work the designs in half cross stitch (page 12) from the charts, leaving one complete thread unworked round each piece (this is the outer row on the charts). Work out from the centre, using one strand of wool or gold ribbon in the tapestry needle and remember that each square on the chart represents one half cross stitch worked over one vertical and one horizontal canvas thread.

Work plain back pieces in half cross stitch using pine green wool, again leaving the unworked thread at the edge.

## MAKING UP

*1 To make each decoration, place a front and back piece together with wrong sides facing. Using the edge thread colour, overcast (page 12) the two pieces together, catching in a jump ring at the top corner.*

*2 Tie thread. Thread 50cm (20in) of ribbon through the jump ring.*

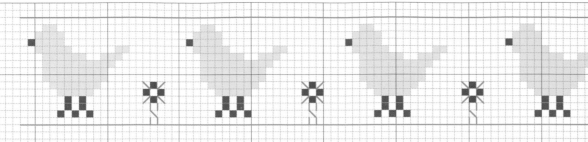

EASTER CAKE BAND

# Cake Band

## WORKBASKET

✤

10cm (4in) wide strip of white 14 count Aida, large enough to fit round your cake, plus 10cm (4in)

✤

1 skein of DMC Stranded Cotton in each of the following colours: yellow 307, grass green 703, orange 971, kingfisher 996

✤

Tapestry needle size 26

✤

Tacking thread in a dark colour

✤

Sewing needle

✤

Two glass-headed pins

## WORKING THE STITCHES

Work a row of tacking down the centre of the strip, lengthways and widthways. Mark the centre of the chart with a soft pencil.

Work the design in cross stitch (page 12) and back stitch (page 12) from the chart. Work outwards from the centre using two strands of thread in the needle throughout and remembering that each coloured square on the chart represents one complete cross stitch worked over one woven block of fabric.

Add an eye to each chick by working a French knot (page 13) using two strands of orange thread in the needle.

## FINISHING THE BAND

**1** *Press the embroidery lightly on the wrong side with a warm iron. Trim*

*away the surplus fabric round the embroidery, leaving three unworked blocks of fabric all round.*

**2** *Using the tapestry needle, gently ease out the threads from the first two woven blocks round the edge of the strip to make a fringe. Press again, then place the band round the cake, overlapping the ends. Secure the band in position with glass-headed pins.*

COLOUR/BACKSTITCH KEY: EASTER

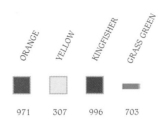

ORANGE — 971
YELLOW — 307
KINGFISHER — 996
GRASS GREEN — 703

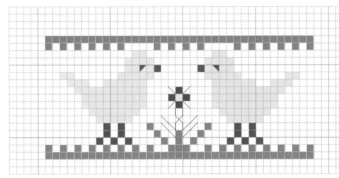

EASTER FLOWERS

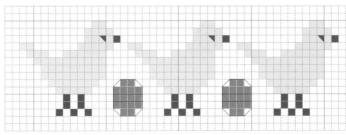

EASTER EGGS

*Cake bands could be used to celebrate many different occasions. Design a band for a special wedding anniversary or embroider one for Christmas which could be used year after year.*

*Celebrate Easter in style by making an embroidered band to decorate an iced cake. Add fluffy chicks and miniature chocolate eggs to the top of the cake.*

# Sampler selection

*Stunning samplers and pleasing pictures add character around the home. Make a teddy picture for the children's bedroom, a motif sampler for the dining or living room, or create your own designs making use of the motifs given throughout the book.*

# Shades of Red

COLOUR/BACKSTITCH KEY: RED SHADES

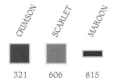

CRIMSON   SCARLET   MAROON

321    606    815

## WORKBASKET

❖

35 x 50cm (14 x 20in)
cream 14 count Aida

❖

DMC Stranded Cotton in the
following colours: 2 skeins
of scarlet 606; 1 skein
each of crimson 321,
maroon 815

❖

Tapestry needle size 24

❖

Embroidery hoop

❖

Tacking thread in a dark colour

❖

Sewing needle

❖

Antique or modern pine
picture frame with aperture
of approximately
15.5 x 33.5cm (6 x 13½in)

❖

Stiff white card and backing board
to fit picture frame

❖

Crochet cotton or piece of
very fine string

❖

Large needle with big eye

❖

Coloured glass-headed
dressmaking pins

❖

Picture framing tacks

❖

Gummed paper strip

## WORKING THE STITCHES

Work a horizontal and vertical
row of tacking stitches across
the fabric to mark the centre
using a dark coloured piece
of thread.

Mark the centre of the main chart with a soft pencil. (You may find it easier to photocopy the charts overleaf, and paste them together.) Mount the centre of the fabric in the embroidery hoop (page 13).

Beginning at the centre, work the design in cross stitch (page 12) from the chart using two strands of thread throughout in the tapestry needle. Each coloured square on the chart represents one complete cross stitch worked over one woven block of Aida fabric.

When all the cross stitch letters have been completed, work the line alphabets from the chart in back stitch (page 12) worked over one block, again using two strands of thread.

Finally, add the back stitch outlines around the block lettering in the same way.

**FINISHING THE SAMPLER**

**1** *Press the embroidery lightly with a warm iron on the wrong side over a well-padded surface, taking care not to crush the stitches. Allow the fabric to cool.*

*Seven alphabets combine to make a stylish sampler embroidered in three shades of red. In addition to stitching the sampler, you could use the alphabets to personalize other cross stitch embroideries, perhaps adding a name and th date to turn a piece of embroidery into a special gift.*

**2** *Position the embroidery centrally over the backing card with the wrong side facing the card. Fold the top of the fabric over the card and check the position of the embroidery in the picture frame. Move the embroidery around at this stage until you are completely happy with the position. Also check the top fold lies along the grain of fabric.*

**3** *Once you are pleased with the fit secure the fold by pushing pins right into the edge of the card. Repeat the process along the bottom edge, taking care to keep the fabric grain straight.*

**4** *Using a long piece of crochet cotton or some very fine string and the large needle, take long stitches between the two fabric edges, starting at the top left. When you have reached the other side, remove the pins.*

**5** *Knot the thread at the starting point, then move downwards from stitch to stitch, tightening the thread as you go. Secure the remaining thread end.*

**6** *Repeat the pinning and lacing process along the remaining two sides of the fabric, ensuring that the corners are folded in neatly. Before pinning check that the folds lie straight along the length of fabric.*

**7** *Frame the embroidery. Place the glass, laced picture and backing board in the frame and fix the layers in place with tacks. Seal the gap between the backing board and the frame using pieces of gummed paper strip.*

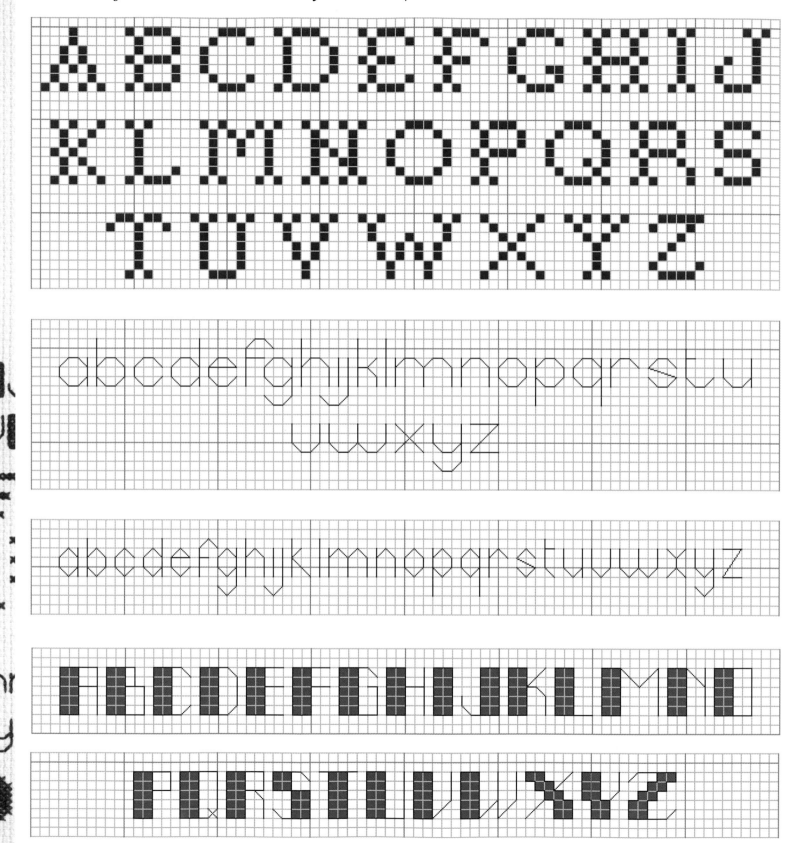

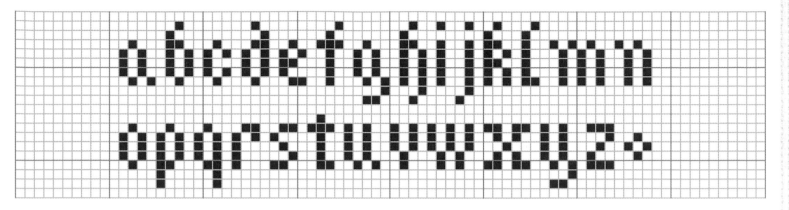

**COMPLETION OF RED SAMPLER (PAGE 66-67)**

**HERB BAGS ALPHABET (PAGES 22-23)**

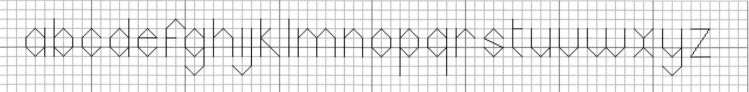

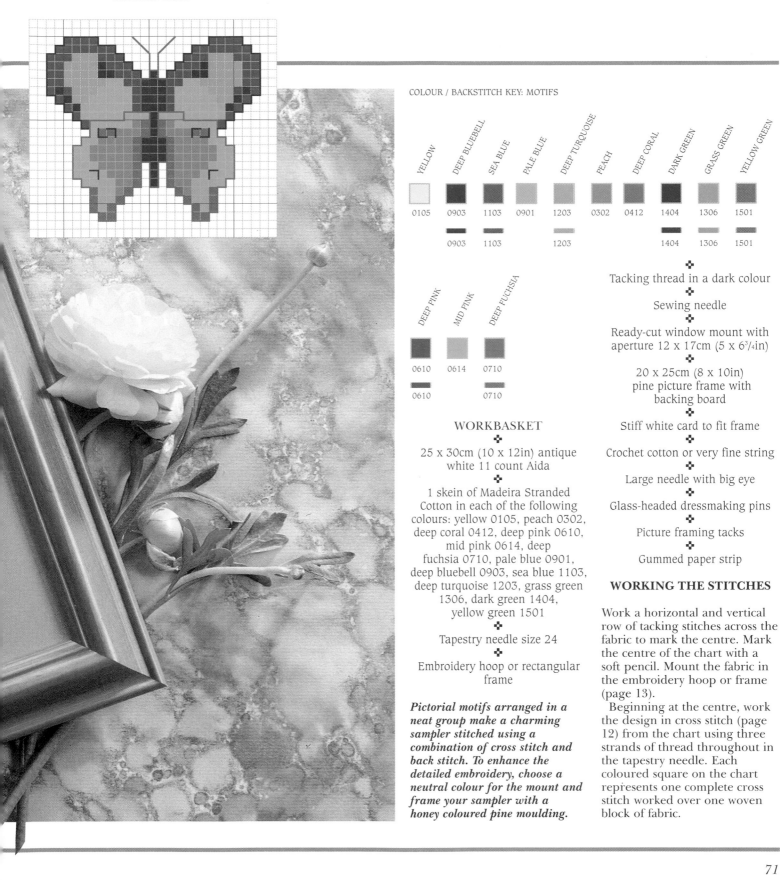

COLOUR / BACKSTITCH KEY: MOTIFS

| YELLOW | DEEP BLUEBELL | SEA BLUE | PALE BLUE | DEEP TURQUOISE | PEACH | DEEP CORAL | DARK GREEN | GRASS GREEN | YELLOW GREEN |
|--------|---------------|----------|-----------|----------------|-------|------------|------------|-------------|--------------|
| 0105 | 0903 | 1103 | 0901 | 1203 | 0302 | 0412 | 1404 | 1306 | 1501 |
| | 0903 | 1103 | | 1203 | | | 1404 | 1306 | 1501 |

| DEEP PINK | MID PINK | DEEP FUCHSIA |
|-----------|----------|--------------|
| 0610 | 0614 | 0710 |
| 0610 | | 0710 |

## WORKBASKET

❖

25 x 30cm (10 x 12in) antique
white 11 count Aida

❖

1 skein of Madeira Stranded
Cotton in each of the following
colours: yellow 0105, peach 0302,
deep coral 0412, deep pink 0610,
mid pink 0614, deep
fuchsia 0710, pale blue 0901,
deep bluebell 0903, sea blue 1103,
deep turquoise 1203, grass green
1306, dark green 1404,
yellow green 1501

❖

Tapestry needle size 24

❖

Embroidery hoop or rectangular
frame

*Pictorial motifs arranged in a
neat group make a charming
sampler stitched using a
combination of cross stitch and
back stitch. To enhance the
detailed embroidery, choose a
neutral colour for the mount and
frame your sampler with a
honey coloured pine moulding.*

❖

Tacking thread in a dark colour

❖

Sewing needle

❖

Ready-cut window mount with
aperture 12 x 17cm (5 x 6³/₄in)

❖

20 x 25cm (8 x 10in)
pine picture frame with
backing board

❖

Stiff white card to fit frame

❖

Crochet cotton or very fine string

❖

Large needle with big eye

❖

Glass-headed dressmaking pins

❖

Picture framing tacks

❖

Gummed paper strip

## WORKING THE STITCHES

Work a horizontal and vertical
row of tacking stitches across the
fabric to mark the centre. Mark
the centre of the chart with a
soft pencil. Mount the fabric in
the embroidery hoop or frame
(page 13).

Beginning at the centre, work
the design in cross stitch (page
12) from the chart using three
strands of thread throughout in
the tapestry needle. Each
coloured square on the chart
represents one complete cross
stitch worked over one woven
block of fabric.

**MOTIF SAMPLER**

When all the cross stitch areas have been completed, add the linear details from the chart working in back stitch (page 12) and working over one block, again using three strands of thread in the needle.

Finally, work a French knot (page 13) at the centre of the fish's eye using three strands of dark green thread.

**FINISHING THE SAMPLER**

**1** *Press the embroidery lightly with a warm iron on the wrong side over a well-padded surface, taking care not to crush the stitches. Allow the fabric to cool.*

**2** *Position the embroidery centrally over the card with the wrong side facing the card. Fold over the top of the fabric and check the position of the embroidery in the mount. Secure the fold with pins pushed right into the edge of the card. Repeat along the bottom edge, taking care to keep the fabric grain straight.*

**3** *Using a piece of crochet cotton or fine string and the large needle, take long stitches between the two edges, starting at the top left. When you have reached the other side, remove the pins. Knot the thread at the start, then move downwards from stitch to stitch, tightening the thread. Secure the other thread end.*

**4** *Repeat the pinning and lacing along the remaining two sides of the fabric, folding in the corners neatly. Place the glass, window mount, laced picture and backing board in the frame and fix the layers in place with tacks. Seal the gap between the backing board and the frame using gummed paper strip.*

**FLEUR-DE-LYS**

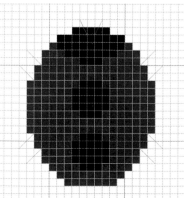

**LADYBIRD**

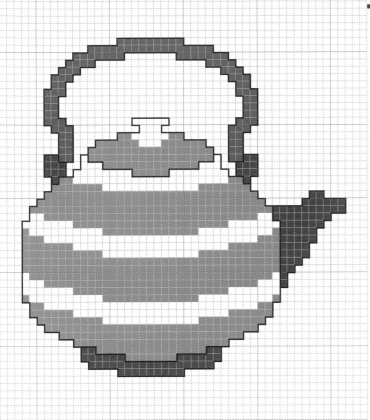

**TEAPOT**

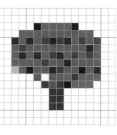

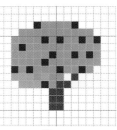

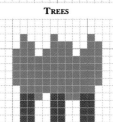

**TREES**

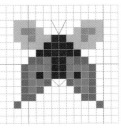

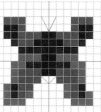

**BEAUTIFUL BUTTERFLIES**

**SAILING LOGO**

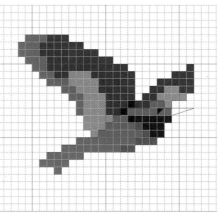

**FLYING FREE**

*Design your own motif sampler by using any combination of these smaller motifs in a pretty group.*

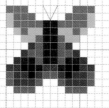

**COUNTRY SCENE**

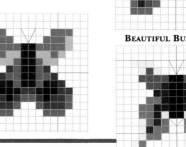

# Framed Flowers

COLOUR / BACKSTITCH KEY: FLOWERS

| PALE CLOVER | DEEP CLOVER | PEACH | CREAM | SOFT BLUE | SAGE GREEN | DEEP GREEN | CHESTNUT | HAZELNUT | BANANA |
|---|---|---|---|---|---|---|---|---|---|
| 776 | 962 | 3824 | 3823 | 3811 | 3816 | 3814 | 3826 | 3828 | 3822 |
| ROSE | | | COLOURS COMMON TO BOTH | | | | DAISY | | |

## WORKBASKET

✤

Two pieces 20 x 20cm (8 x 8in) cream 11 count Aida

✤

1 skein of DMC Stranded Cotton in each of the following colours: pale clover 776, deep clover 962, soft blue 3811, deep green 3814, sage green 3816, banana 3822, cream 3823, peach 3824, chestnut 3826, hazelnut 3828

✤

Tapestry needle size 24

✤

Small embroidery hoop

✤

Tacking thread in a dark colour

✤

Sewing needle

✤

Pair of brass picture frames with aperture 8 x 8cm (3½ x 3½in)

✤

Two pieces of stiff white card to fit picture frame

✤

Crochet cotton or very fine string

✤

Large needle with big eye

✤

Glass-headed dressmaking pins

## WORKING THE STITCHES

Work a horizontal and vertical row of tacking stitches across each piece of fabric to mark the centre. Mark the centre of each chart with a soft pencil. Mount the centre of one piece of fabric in the hoop (page 13).

Beginning at the centre, work the rose design in cross stitch (page 12) from the chart using three strands of thread throughout in the tapestry needle. Each coloured square on the chart represents one complete cross stitch worked over one woven block of fabric.

When all the cross stitch areas have been completed, work the linear details from the chart in back stitch (page 12) worked over one block, again using three strands of thread.

Repeat the process to embroider the daisy picture.

## FINISHING THE PICTURES

**1** *Press the finished embroideries lightly with a warm iron on the wrong side over a well-padded surface, taking care not to crush the stitches. Allow the fabric to cool.*

**2** *Position one embroidery centrally over one piece of card with the wrong side facing the card. Carefully fold over the top of the fabric and check the position of the embroidery with the picture frame. Secure the fold with pins pushed right into the edge of the card. Repeat along the bottom edge, taking care to keep the fabric grain straight.*

**3** *Using a long piece of crochet cotton and the large needle, take long stitches between the edges, starting at the top left. Then, remove the pins.*

**FLORAL DAISY & FLORAL ROSE**

*Stitch a pair of pretty floral motifs and show them off with matching plain brass frames. Here, a selection of subtle thread shades have been used for the embroidery but you could ring the changes if you prefer and use brighter colours for both flowers and backgrounds.*

# Monogram Picture

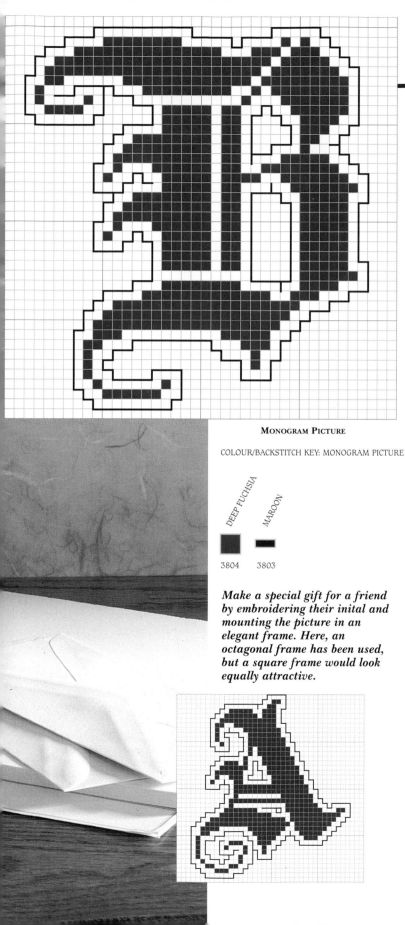

**MONOGRAM PICTURE**

COLOUR/BACKSTITCH KEY: MONOGRAM PICTURE

DEEP FUCHSIA    MAROON

3804    3803

*Make a special gift for a friend by embroidering their inital and mounting the picture in an elegant frame. Here, an octagonal frame has been used, but a square frame would look equally attractive.*

## WORKBASKET

❖

20 x 20cm (8 x 8in) cream 11 count Aida

❖

1 skein of DMC Stranded Cotton in each of the following colours: maroon 3803, deep fuchsia 3804

❖

Tapestry needle size 24

❖

Embroidery hoop or rectangular frame

❖

Tacking thread in a dark colour

❖

Sewing needle

❖

Octagonal picture frame

❖

Window mount with circular aperture 10cm (4in) in diameter

❖

Stiff white card to fit picture frame

❖

Crochet cotton or very fine string

❖

Large needle with big eye

❖

Glass-headed dressmaking pins

## WORKING THE STITCHES

Work a horizontal and vertical row of tacking stitches across the fabric to mark the centre. Mark the centre of the chart showing your chosen letter with a soft pencil. Mount the centre of the fabric in the hoop or frame (page 13).

Beginning at the centre, work the letter in cross stitch (page 12) from the chart, given here or overleaf, using three strands of thread throughout in the tapestry needle.

Each coloured square on the chart represents one complete cross stitch worked over one woven block of fabric.

When all the cross stitch areas have been completed, work the outline from the chart in back stitch (page 12), again working each stitch over one block, and using three strands of thread in the needle.

## FINISHING THE PICTURE

**1** *Press the embroidery lightly with a warm iron on the wrong side over a well-padded surface, taking care not to crush the stitches. Allow the fabric to cool.*

**2** *Position the embroidery centrally over the card with the wrong side facing the card. Fold over the top of the fabric and check the position of the embroidery using the frame's window mount.*

**3** *Secure the fold with pins pushed right into the edge of the card. Repeat the process along the bottom edge, taking care to keep the fabric grain straight.*

**4** *Using a long piece of crochet cotton or a very fine length of string and the large needle, take long stitches between the two fabric edges,*

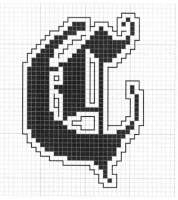

77

starting at the top left. When you
have reached the other side, remove
the pins. Knot the thread at the
starting point, then move
downwards from stitch to stitch,
tightening the thread as you go.
Secure the remaining thread end.

**5** Repeat the pinning and lacing
along the two lower edges of the
fabric, folding in the corners neatly,
then repeat along the remaining four
sides of the octagon. Place the glass,
laced picture and backing board in
the frame and tightly
fasten the closures.

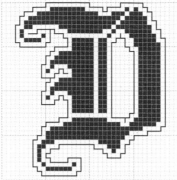
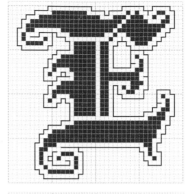
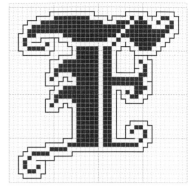

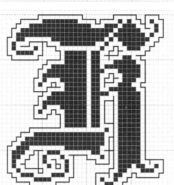
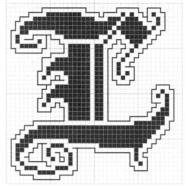
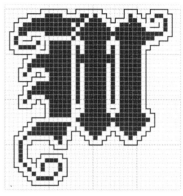

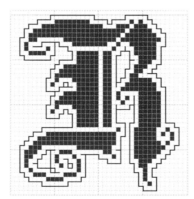
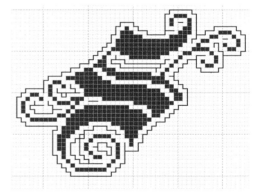

*This amazing Gothic-style
alphabet could be used for
initalizing any number of items
around the home. If you were
feeling adventurous you might
even consider making a
tablecloth using the motifs – then
have a Mad Hatter's tea party!*

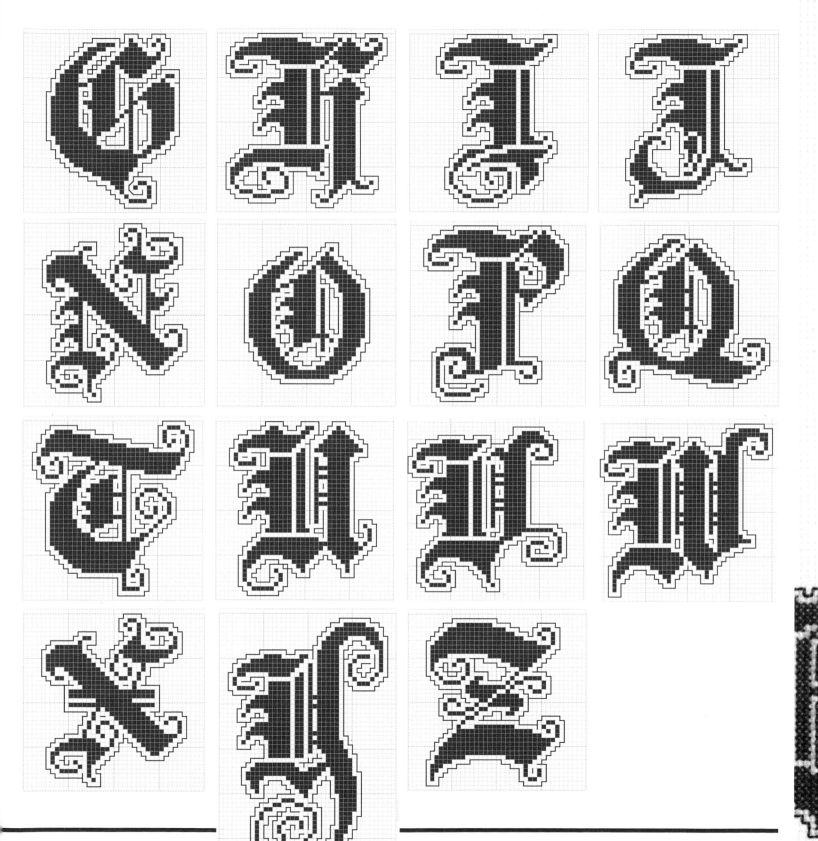

# Teddy Treats

## WORKBASKET

❖

25 x 30cm (10 x 12in) antique white 14 count Aida

❖

DMC Stranded Cotton in the following colours:
2 skeins of shaded brown 61;
1 skein each of white, dark grey 413, scarlet 606, dark brown 938, kingfisher 996, pink 3779

❖

Tapestry needle size 24

❖

Embroidery hoop or rectangular frame

❖

Tacking thread in a dark colour

❖

Sewing needle

❖

Plain wooden picture frame with aperture 17 x 12cm
(6³⁄₄ x 4³⁄₄in)

❖

Stiff white card and backing board to fit picture frame

❖

Crochet cotton or very fine string

❖

Large needle with big eye

❖

Glass-headed dressmaking pins

❖

Picture framing tacks

❖

Gummed paper strip

## WORKING THE STITCHES

Work a horizontal and vertical row of tacking stitches across the fabric to mark the centre. Mark the centre of the chart with a soft pencil. Mount the fabric in the hoop or frame (page 13).

Beginning at the centre, work the teddy design in cross stitch (page 12) from the chart using

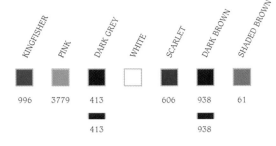

COLOUR/BACKSTITCH KEY: TEDDY TREATS

| KINGFISHER | PINK | DARK GREY | WHITE | SCARLET | DARK BROWN | SHADED BROWN |
|---|---|---|---|---|---|---|
| 996 | 3779 | 413 | | 606 | 938 | 61 |
| | | 413 | | | 938 | |

*This pair of sprightly teddy bears would make a delightful decoration for a child's room. Stitched in shaded and solid-coloured threads, the teddies and balloons are easy to work and you could add a title beneath the motifs using one of the cross stitch alphabets shown on page 66.*

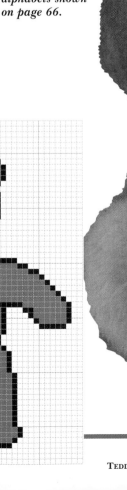

**TEDDY PICTURE**

three strands of embroidery thread throughout in the tapestry needle. Each coloured square on the chart represents one complete cross stitch worked over one woven block of fabric.

When all the cross stitch areas have been completed, add the linear details from the chart in back stitch (page 12) worked over one block, again using three strands of thread.

### FINISHING THE PICTURE

**1** *Press the embroidery lightly with a warm iron on the wrong side over a well-padded surface, taking care not to crush the stitches. Allow the fabric to cool.*

**2** *Position the embroidery centrally over the card with the wrong side facing the card. Fold over the top of the fabric and check the position of the embroidery with the window mount. Secure the fold with pins pushed right into the edge of the card. Repeat along the bottom edge, taking care to keep the fabric grain straight.*

**3** *Using a long piece of crochet cotton or fine string and the large needle, take long stitches between the two fabric edges, starting at the top left. When you have reached the other side, remove the pins. Knot the thread at the starting point, then move downwards from stitch to stitch, tightening the thread as you go. Tightly secure the remaining thread end.*

**4** *Repeat the pinning and lacing along the remaining two sides of the fabric, folding in the corners neatly, and checking the edges are straight. Place the glass, window mount, laced picture and backing board in the frame and fix the layers in place with tacks. Seal the gap between the backing board and the frame using gummed paper strip.*

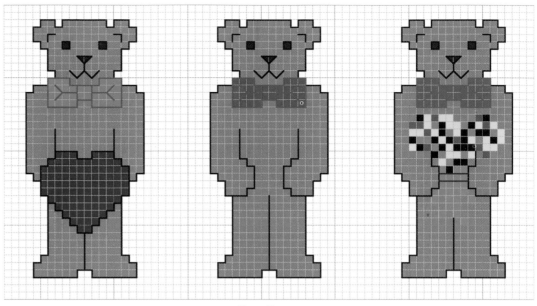

PARTY TIME

*Cuddly teddies are always firm favourites with both adults and children, and the bears here are sure to bring a smile to anyone's face.*

*The smaller motifs could be used on clothes, while the larger bear motifs would be perfect for blankets, towels, pictures and samplers.*

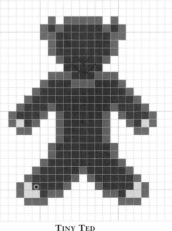

TINY TED

CUDDLY TED

**BIRTHDAY TIME**

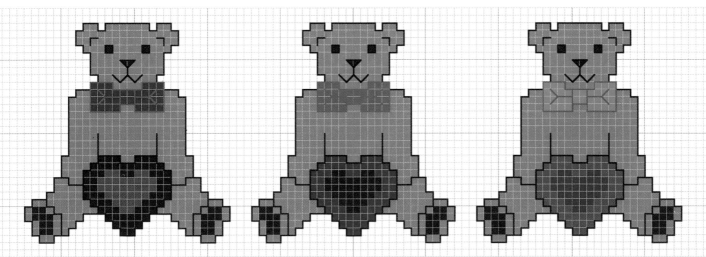

**LOVING BEARS**

## WORKBASKET

✤

50 x 60cm (20 x 24in) antique white 11 count Aida

✤

1 skein of Caron Collection Wildflowers thread in each of the following colours: peach melba 021, fuchsia 037, flame 045, emerald 065, jade 066, woodlands 076, african sunset 084, blue spruce 091

✤

Tapestry needle size 24

✤

Large embroidery hoop

✤

Tacking thread in a dark colour

✤

Sewing needle

✤

Ready-cut window mount with aperture 27.5 x 34.5cm (11 x 14in)

✤

Picture frame with backing board

✤

Stiff white card to fit picture frame

✤

Crochet cotton or very fine string

✤

Large needle with big eye

✤

Glass-headed dressmaking pins

✤

Picture framing tacks

✤

Gummed paper strip

*Based on traditional Elizabethan patterns, this sampler features bands of stylized flowers and leaves worked in delicate shades of pink and green using hand-dyed cotton threads.*

## WORKING THE STITCHES

Work a horizontal and vertical row of tacking stitches across the fabric to mark the centre. Mark the centre of the chart with a soft pencil. Mount the centre of the fabric in the hoop (page 13).

Beginning at the centre, work the design in cross stitch (page 12) from the chart using one strand of thread throughout in the tapestry needle. Each coloured square on the chart represents one complete cross stitch worked over one woven block of fabric. When finished, each embroidered band should extend about 1.5cm (¹/₂in) at each side beyond the aperture of the window mount.

When all the cross stitch areas have been completed, add the linear details from the chart in back stitch (page 12) worked over one block, again using one strand of thread. The back stitch lines are indicted in black on the chart, but they should be worked in the same thread colour as the adjacent cross stitches.

## FINISHING THE SAMPLER

**1** Press the embroidery lightly with a warm iron on the wrong side over a well-padded surface, taking care not to crush the stitches. Allow the fabric to cool.

**2** Position the embroidery centrally over the card with the wrong side facing the card. Fold over the top of the fabric and check the position of the embroidery with the window mount. Secure the fold with pins pushed right into the edge of the card. Repeat along the bottom edge, taking care to keep the fabric grain straight.

**3** Using a long piece of crochet cotton or very fine string and the large needle, take long stitches between the two fabric edges, starting at the top left. When you have reached the other side, remove the pins. Knot the thread at the starting point, then move downwards from stitch to stitch, tightening the thread as you go. Secure the remaining thread end.

**4** Repeat the pinning and lacing along the remaining two sides of the fabric, folding in the corners neatly. Place the glass, window mount, laced picture and backing board in the frame and fix the layers in place with tacks. Seal the gap between the backing board and the frame using gummed paper strip.

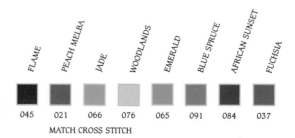

COLOUR / BACKSTITCH KEY: TRADITIONAL IDEAS

| FLAME | PEACH MELBA | JADE | WOODLANDS | EMERALD | BLUE SPRUCE | AFRICAN SUNSET | FUCHSIA |
|-------|-------------|------|-----------|---------|-------------|----------------|---------|
| 045 | 021 | 066 | 076 | 065 | 091 | 084 | 037 |

MATCH CROSS STITCH

ELIZABETHAN SAMPLER

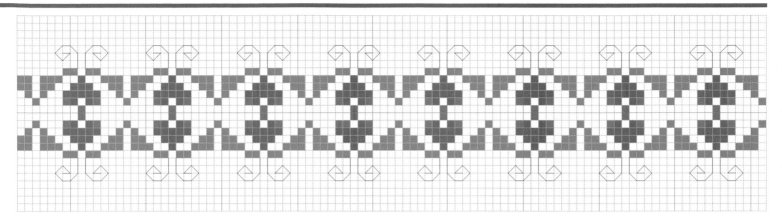

**DELICATE BOWS**

**ALL LINED UP**

**BORDER IDEAS**

*These designs could be used as alternatives in this sampler. Simply replace one line of the chart with another.*

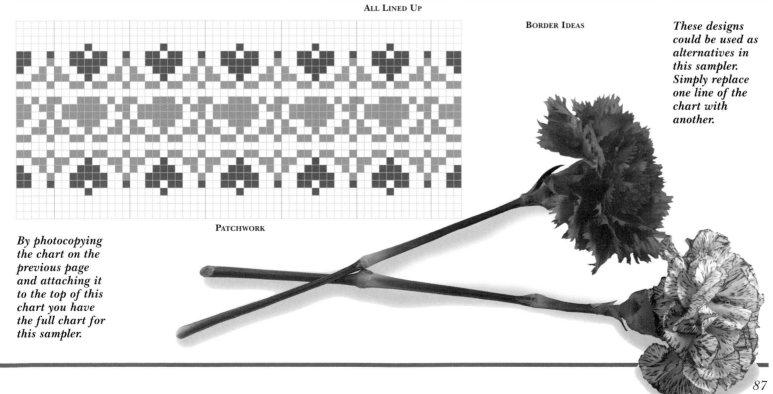

**PATCHWORK**

*By photocopying the chart on the previous page and attaching it to the top of this chart you have the full chart for this sampler.*

# Photo Surround

design in cross stitch (page 12)

## WORKBASKET

❖

Piece of brown perforated
embroidery paper to fit the
picture frame

❖

1 skein of DMC Stranded
Cotton in each of the
following colours: hyacinth 340,
lichen green 581, grass
green 703, oak brown 829,
deep ochre 832, lime green 907,
light emerald 911, rust 920,
light tan 922, pine green 3818,
yellow green 3819

❖

Tapestry needle size 24

❖

Tacking thread in a dark colour

❖

Painted wooden standing frame
with aperture 12 x 17cm
(4³/₄ x 7in)

❖

Stiff black card and backing
board cut to size to fit the
picture frame

❖

Masking tape

❖

Sharp scissors

## WORKING THE STITCHES

Using the dark coloured thread,
work a horizontal and vertical
row of tacking stitches across the
brown perforated paper to mark
the centre.

Mark a cross to show the
centre of the cross stitch chart
with a soft coloured pencil.

Working outwards from the
centre, work the landscape

design in cross stitch (page 12)
from the chart using three
strands of thread throughout in
the tapestry needle.

Each coloured square on the
chart represents one complete
cross stitch worked over one
'thread' on the perforated
paper.

## FINISHING THE FRAME

**1** *Using the sharp scissors carefully
cut out the central area of the
brown perforated paper, leaving
a margin of one unworked paper
'thread' all round the embroidered
design.*

**2** *Lay the perforated paper over the
black backing card and lightly mark
around the position of the cut-out
aperture using a soft pencil.*

**3** *Centre the photograph face up
over these pencil lines so that the
main image is between these lines.
Check you are happy with the
position of the main image.*

**4** *Then, carefully secure the
photograph in position on the card
using tiny strips of masking tape
round the edge.*

**5** *Frame the picture and design.
Place the glass, embroidered
paper frame, card with attached
photograph and backing board in the
frame all right side up and
facing outwards, and tightly fasten
the closures. The photograph and
frame is now ready to be displayed in
the home.*

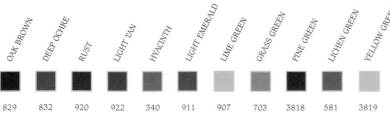

PHOTOGRAPH SURROUND

*Perforated paper and
subtle shades of blue,
brown and green threads
combined with a
landscape design make
an unusual surrounding
for a treasured antique
photograph.*

*Make sure you use
a pair of sharp
scissors with fine points
when cutting out the
shaped aperture for
the photograph.*

COLOUR KEY: PHOTO SURROUND

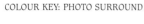

| OAK BROWN | DEEP OCHRE | RUST | LIGHT TAN | HYACINTH | LIGHT EMERALD | LIME GREEN | GRASS GREEN | PINE GREEN | LICHEN GREEN | YELLOW GREEN |
|---|---|---|---|---|---|---|---|---|---|---|
| 829 | 832 | 920 | 922 | 340 | 911 | 907 | 703 | 3818 | 581 | 3819 |

# Cutting a dash

*Add style to your favourite outfits with designer buttons
worked in geometric designs, make your own jewellery
and even monogram your hankies all with cross stitch.
Once you have the knack why not embroider other items
like blouse and shirt collars?*

# Beautiful Buttons

## WORKBASKET

✤

Scraps of cream 11 count and 18 count Aida

✤

1 skein of DMC Cotton in dark grey 413

✤

Tapestry needle size 26

✤

29mm (1in) and 22mm (³/₄in) brass-rimmed button moulds

✤

Fine-point black felt pen with permanent ink

### PREPARING THE FABRIC

*1 Place the fabric scraps on a flat surface. Remove the piece of backing card from one of the button moulds, place it on a piece of fabric and draw round it with the felt pen – this marks the cutting line.*

*2 Repeat for the desired number of buttons. Mark the centre of each chart with a soft pencil.*

### WORKING THE STITCHES

Work the designs from the charts in cross stitch (page 12). Work outwards from the centre of each design until the cutting line is reached and remember that each coloured square on the chart represents one complete cross stitch worked over one woven block of fabric.

Use two strands of thread in the needle for 18 count fabric and three strands for 11 count fabric.

### FINISHING THE BUTTONS

*1 Press the finished embroideries very lightly on the wrong side with a cool iron. Press each piece over a well-padded surface and take care not to flatten the stitches.*

*2 Cut out each embroidery along the circular outline. Assemble the layers*

*of the mould on a flat surface – holder, brass rim, embroidery (right side downwards) metal centre, back and finally the pusher. Push the pusher firmly downwards to secure all the layers.*

**Geometric centre patterns worked in one dark shade of thread on cream fabric make stylish centrepieces for brass-rimmed button moulds. Vary the appearance of the buttons by altering the fabric count, size of button mould and also by varying the weight of your thread.**

COLOUR KEY: BEAUTIFUL BUTTONS

■ DARK GREY 413

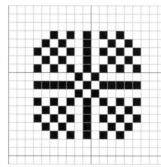

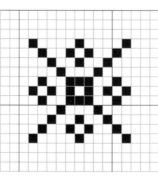

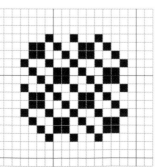

Use one or all of these designs for your buttons, and ring the changes by using different coloured threads.

# Scattered Strawberries

## WORKBASKET

❖

6 x 6cm (2¹/₂ x 2¹/₂in) pieces of 10 mesh waste canvas, one for each strawberry

❖

DMC Stranded Cotton in the following colours: yellow 307, scarlet 606, green 702 (1 skein of each colour will work about twelve strawberries)

❖

Crewel needle size 8

❖

Tacking thread in a light colour

❖

Sewing needle and pins

❖

Child's denim dress

## PREPARING THE DRESS

**1** *Randomly pin squares of waste canvas on the front of the skirt and sleeves of the dress. When you are happy with the arrangement, tack each square securely to the fabric and mark the square's centres with a few tacking stitches.*

**2** *Turn the dress over and add canvas squares to the back skirt and sleeves tacking them on in the same way. Mark the centre of the two strawberry charts with a soft pencil.*

## WORKING THE STITCHES

Work the embroidery from the two strawberry charts in cross stitch (page 12) using three strands of thread in the crewel needle throughout.

*Strawberry motifs add interest to a child's denim dress. The motifs are quick and easy to embroider – each stitch is worked through both canvas and fabric, then the canvas threads are removed. Scatter the strawberries randomly on the skirt and sleeves of the dress.*

**STRAWBERRY MOTIF**

COLOUR KEY: SCATTERED STRAWBERRIES

SCARLET | YELLOW | GREEN

606 | 307 | 702

Work outwards from the centre of the design remembering that each coloured square on the chart represents one complete cross stitch worked over one vertical and one horizontal double thread of canvas.

### FINISHING THE DRESS

**1** *Press the embroidery lightly on the wrong side over a well-padded surface. Remove the canvas threads. Use tweezers and pull each thread out individually.*

*Why not make a set of napkins or hankies and give each one a different motif?*

**PLUMS**

**APPLES**

**CHERRIES**

# Embroidered Apron

**WORKBASKET**

✛

16 x 16cm (6¹⁄₂ x 6¹⁄₂in)
antique white 14
count Aida

✛

1 skein of DMC
Stranded Cotton in each
of the following colours:
deep red 321, reddish
brown 351, scarlet 606,
grass green 704, orange 741,
light emerald 911,
cream 3823, pale gold 3828

✛

Tapestry needle size 26

✛

Small embroidery hoop

✛

Tacking thread in a dark colour

✛

Sewing needle

✛

Paper pattern for apron

✛

Red and white gingham fabric

✛

Red bias binding

✛

Red and cream sewing thread

## WORKING THE STITCHES

Using a dark coloured thread work a horizontal and vertical row of tacking stitches across the evenweave fabric to mark the centre.

Mark the centre of the cross stitch chart with a soft pencil.

Mount the evenweave fabric in the embroidery hoop (page 13).

Beginning at the centre, work the design in cross stitch (page 12) from the chart using two strands of embroidery thread throughout in the tapestry needle.

Each coloured square on the chart represents one complete cross stitch worked over one woven block of fabric.

When all the cross stitch areas have been completed, add the linear details from the chart in

back stitch (page 12) worked over one woven block of fabric, again using two strands of embroidery thread in the tapestry needle.

*Mouthwatering vegetable motifs, arranged in neat rows, decorate an embroidered pocket and make a simple red and white gingham apron into something special for the kitchen.*

*Choose a plain pattern for the apron, neaten the fabric edges and make the neck band and ties from plain red bias binding.*

COLOUR / BACKSTITCH KEY:
EMBROIDERED APRON

| PALE GOLD | CREAM | ORANGE | DEEP RED | SCARLET |
|---|---|---|---|---|
| 3828 | 3823 | 741 | 321 | 606 |
| 3828 | | | 321 | |

| REDDISH BROWN | GRASS GREEN | LIGHT EMERALD |
|---|---|---|
| 351 | 704 | 911 |

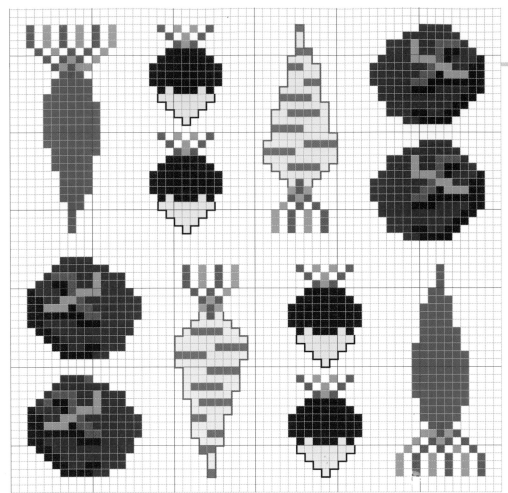

**APRON POCKET**

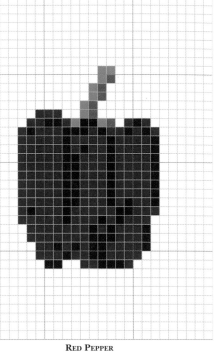

**RED PEPPER**

## MAKING UP THE APRON

**1** *Press the embroidery lightly with a warm iron on the wrong side over a well-padded surface, taking care not to crush the stitches. Allow the fabric to cool.*

**2** *Pin the paper pattern on the gingham and cut out. Bind the top of the embroidered pocket with bias binding. Turn under 1.5cm (¹/₂in) along the remaining three sides and tack in place.*

**3** *Bind the raw edges of the apron with bias binding - bind the armhole edges first, then along the top edge and finally round the remaining of the body of the apron.*

**4** *Make the ties and neck strap by folding lengths of bias binding*

*in half widthways and machine stitching close to the edge with red sewing thread. Attach the ties and strap securely to the apron.*

**5** *Pin the pocket on to the apron and try it on to check the position. Tack and machine stitch to the apron using cream sewing thread.*

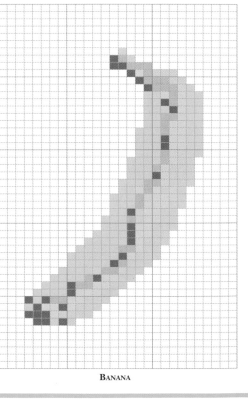

**BANANA**

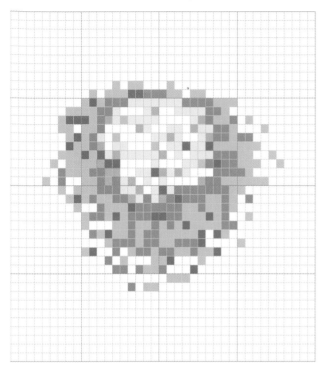

**CAULIFLOWER**

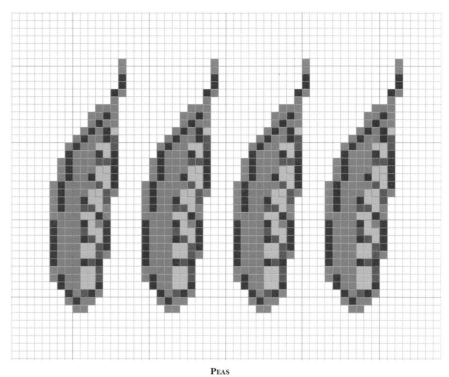

**PEAS**

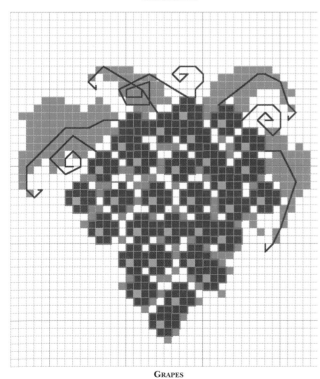

**GRAPES**

Other vegetables
could be
included in this
design, or could
be used for
alternative items
around the
kitchen.
Why not add
apples and grapes
to the tea towels,
and use the peas
or the
cauliflower on a
pair of oven
gloves?
If you prefer use
the radishes or
carrots on your
kitchen items.

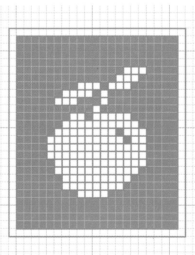

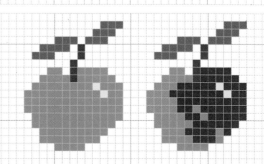

# Fancy Hankies

## WORKBASKET

✦

6 x 6cm (2¹⁄₂ x 2¹⁄₂in) piece of 14 mesh waste canvas for each initial

✦

1 skein of DMC Stranded Cotton in airforce blue 3807 - this amount will embroider several handkerchiefs

✦

Crewel needle size 9

✦

Tacking thread in a light colour

✦

Sewing needle and pins

✦

White linen handkerchiefs

## PREPARING THE HANKIES

**1** *Pin a square of waste canvas at the corner of each handkerchief. Tack each square securely to the fabric and mark the centre with a few tacking stitches.*

**2** *Mark the centre of your chosen charted letter with a soft pencil.*

## WORKING THE STITCHES

Work the embroidery from the chart in cross stitch (page 12) using two strands of thread in the crewel needle throughout.

Work outwards from the centre of the design remembering that each coloured square on the chart represents one complete cross stitch worked over one vertical and one horizontal double thread of canvas.

## FINISHING THE HANKIES

**1** *Press the embroidery lightly on the wrong side over a well-padded surface to set the stitches. Remove the canvas threads using tweezers (page 13).*

*Fabric handkerchiefs look stylish, particularly when they are made from the finest white Irish linen and decorated with a fancy initial embroidered in cross stitch. The initials are quick and easy to work using the waste canvas method.*

### INITIALS FOR HANKIES

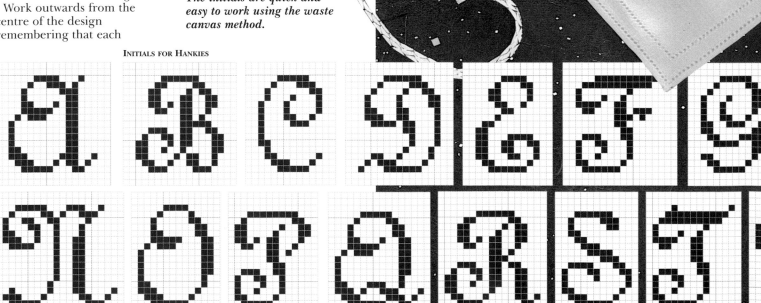

Other alphabets will work well on hankies. Try the alphabet on pages 30-31, or use one of the characters given on page 68-69. Small designs can also be used on hankies, perhaps a small strawberry motif from page 94-95.

**BUTTERFLY**

**STRAWBERRY**

**ICE CREAM**

THE SMALL MOTIFS SHOWN HERE ARE TAKEN FROM PAGES 30-31 & 95

# Flower Jewellery

## WORKBASKET

✦

Scraps of white 8 count and 11 count Aida

✦

1 skein of DMC Cotton in each of the following colours: grass green 704, lime green 907, deep fuchsia 3804, fuchsia 3606, sage green 3816, deep banana 3821, peach 3824

✦

Tapestry needle size 24

✦

Silver-plated jewellery mounts from Framecraft (page 108)

✦

Fine-point black felt pen with permanent ink

COLOUR KEY: FLOWER JEWELLERY

| SAGE GREEN | GRASS GREEN | LIME GREEN | FUCHSIA | PEACH |
|---|---|---|---|---|
| 3816 | 704 | 907 | 3806 | 3824 |

| DEEP FUCHSIA | DEEP BANANA |
|---|---|
| 3804 | 3821 |

## PREPARING THE FABRIC

1 *Place the fabric scraps on a flat surface. Remove the piece of acetate from one of the jewellery mounts, place it on a piece of fabric and draw round it with the felt pen – this marks the cutting line. Repeat for each mount.*

## WORKING THE STITCHES

Using the photograph as a guide, embroider the designs in cross stitch (page 12). Work one or more flowerheads from the chart then add details in running stitch and back stitch (page 12). The chart also gives four different colour combinations for you to use. Work outwards from the centre until the cutting line is reached and remember that each coloured square on the chart represents one complete cross stitch worked over one woven block of fabric. Use three strands of thread in the needle for 11 count fabric and six strands for 8 count fabric.

## FINISHING OFF

1 *Press the finished embroideries very lightly on the wrong side with a cool iron. Press each piece over a well-padded surface and take care not to flatten the stitches.*

2 *Cut out each embroidery along the cutting line and frame in the silver-plated mounts following the manufacturer's instructions.*

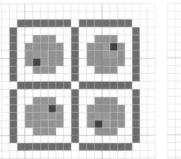

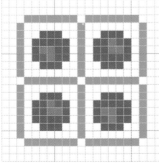

JEWELLERY MOTIFS

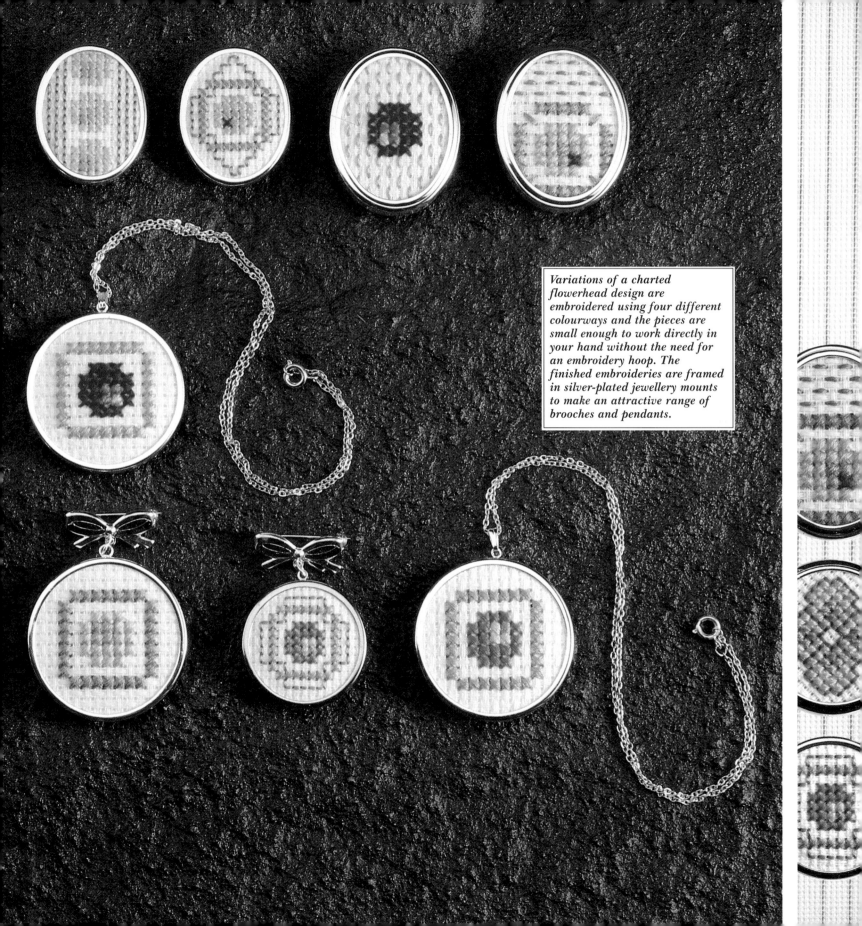

*Variations of a charted flowerhead design are embroidered using four different colourways and the pieces are small enough to work directly in your hand without the need for an embroidery hoop. The finished embroideries are framed in silver-plated jewellery mounts to make an attractive range of brooches and pendants.*

# Favourite Handbag

## WORKBASKET

❖

30 x 20cm (12 x 8in) of Christmas green 11 count Aida

❖

1 skein of DMC Stranded Cotton in each of the following colours: pale pink 605, pale turquoise 959, kingfisher 995, pale kingfisher 996, dark grey 3799, maroon 3803, mid pink 3805, jade green 3812, mid green 3815, deep green 3818,

mid gold 3826, pale gold 3828, rust 3830

❖

Tapestry needle size 24

❖

Crewel needle size 9

❖

Small embroidery hoop

❖

Tacking thread in a light colour

❖

Matching sewing thread

❖

Sewing needle and pins

❖

Pack of gold 00557 Mill Hill glass seed beads

❖

Two pieces 26 x 35cm (10¼ x 14in) of dark green silk dupion

❖

Pair of gold-coloured cord tie-backs with large tassels

❖

Fusible bonding web

❖

Knitting needle

*A dark green silk bag with an applied panel of cross stitch paisley designs opens and closes by means of a pair of cord tie-backs. The edges of the embroidered panel are decorated with a row of gold seed beads.*

COLOUR / BACKSTITCH KEY:
FAVOURITE HANDBAG

| PALE GOLD | MID GOLD | RUST | JADE GREEN | MID GREEN |
|---|---|---|---|---|
| 3828 | 3826 | 3830 | 3812 | 3815 |

| DEEP GREEN | PALE PINK | MID PINK | MAROON | PALE TURQUOISE |
|---|---|---|---|---|
| 3818 | 605 | 3805 | 3803 | 959 |

| PALE KINGFISHER | KINGFISHER | DARK GREY |
|---|---|---|
| 996 | 995 | 3799 |

## WORKING THE STITCHES

Work a horizontal and vertical row of tacking stitches across the embroidery fabric to mark the centre. Mark the centre of the chart with a soft pencil. Mount the fabric in the embroidery hoop (page 13).

Beginning at the centre, work the paisley design in cross stitch (page 12) from the chart using three strands of thread throughout in the tapestry needle.

Each coloured square on the chart represents one complete cross stitch worked over one woven block of fabric.

When all the cross stitch areas have been completed, add the linear details from the chart in back stitch (page 12) worked over one block, again using three strands of thread.

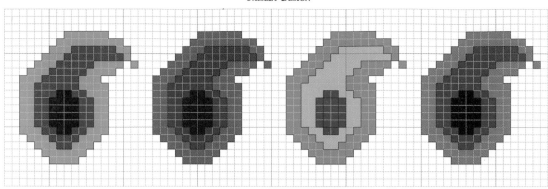

*Paisley teardrops are lovely design shapes, and work perfectly on this handbag. They will also make good motifs on other items of clothing, shirt collars, tee-shirts and even as patches on trousers.*

## ATTACHING THE MOTIFS

**1** *Press the embroidery lightly with a warm iron on the wrong side over a well-padded surface, taking care not to crush the stitches. Following the manufacturer's instructions, iron a piece of fusible bonding web on to the back of the embroidery. When cool, cut away the surplus fabric, leaving a margin of six unworked blocks of fabric round the design.*

**2** *Peel away the backing paper from the embroidery and position towards the bottom of one piece of silk, about 8cm (3in) from the lower edge and an equal distance from each side. Press with a steam iron (or an ordinary iron and a damp cloth) to attach the embroidered panel.*

**3** *Work a row of blanket stitch (page 12) round the panel using two stands of deep green thread in the crewel needle and making each stitch two woven blocks high. Using the same thread and needle, work a row of back stitch (page 12) round the panel, attaching one bead with every stitch. Position the row of back stitches two blocks from the edge.*

## MAKING UP THE BAG

**1** *Place the two pieces of silk together with right sides facing and pin together round the edge. Machine stitch across the base and up the two sides, taking a 1.5cm (¹/2in) seam allowance and stopping the stitching at each side 13cm (5in) from the top edge. Trim away some of the surplus fabric round the lower corners and turn the bag to the right side, pushing each corner out gently with the knitting needle.*

**2** *Press the side seams lightly with a warm iron, folding over and pressing the seam allowance right to the top of the bag. Turn over 1.5cm (¹/2in) along both the top edges and press. Turn over both top edges until the top fold reaches the point where the side seam stops. Tack along the folds and machine stitch in place. Work a second row of stitching 2cm (³/4in) above the first, making a channel on the back and the front to accommodate the cord.*

**3** *Cut one tie-back in half at the end opposite the tassel. Thread the cut ends through the back and front channels and tie the two ends firmly in a knot, leaving about 15cm (6in) of cord free beyond the knot. Fringe the cut ends, knotting each strand separately. Repeat with the second tie-back, threading it in the other direction through the channels so that the two tassels emerge on opposite sides of the bag. Pull the tassels to close the bag.*

**TWISTED SQUARE**

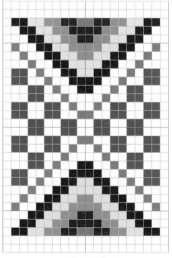

**INSIDE OUT**

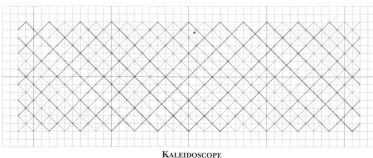

**KALEIDOSCOPE**

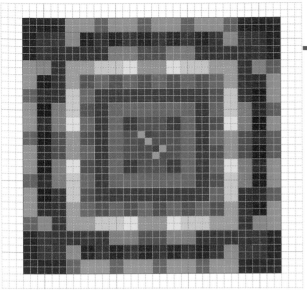

**CHECKERS**

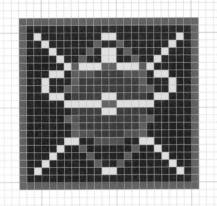

**WOMBAT**

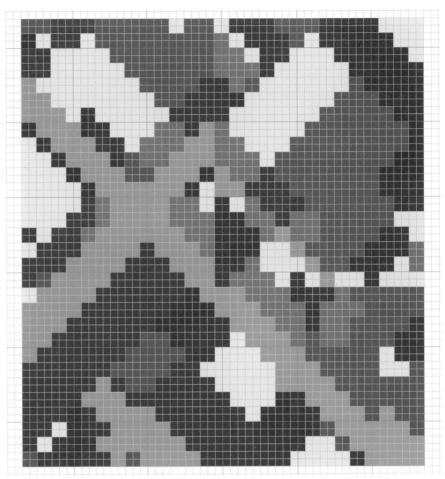

**RANDOM COLOURS**

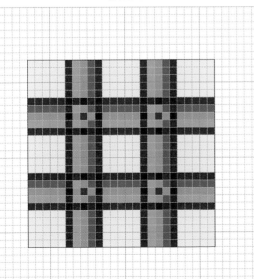

**SCOTCH QUILT**

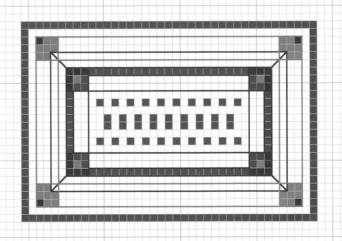

**HI-TEC**

## Acknowledgements

Cara Ackerman, Gavin Fry, Sarah Gray, Lesley Harmer, Bea Neilson, Helen Stuttle for all their help

DMC Creative World Ltd, Pullman Road, Wigston, Leicestershire, LE18 2DY, for supplying embroidery threads
(except pages 24/25, 70/71, 84/85) and embroidery fabrics
Coats Craft UK, McMullen Road, Darlington, Co Durham, DL1 1YQ, for Anchor and Kreinik
embroidery threads
Readicut Craft Collection, for Madeira embroidery threads
Macleod Craft Marketing, West Yonderton, Warlock Road, Bridge of Weir, Renfrewshire, PA11 3SR, for Caron
Collection embroidery threads
Framecraft Mail Order from Framecraft Miniatures Ltd, 372-376 Summer Lane, Hockley, Birmingham, B19 3QA,
for the jewellery boxes, Mill Hill beads, mounts and address books
Panda Ribbons, for the ribbons and piping
Siesta Interlocking Frames, PO Box 1759, Ferndown, Dorset, BH22 8YR
Nigel Benson for the antique picture frames
Ian and Martin Lawson-Smith at IL-Soft
Crafts Beautiful for kind permission to use the designs on page 18/19, 56/57, 66/67
Classic Stitches for kind permission to use the designs on pages 84/85

The endpapers of this book show a selection of colours from the full range of DMC Stranded Cotton

## CREDITS

**Managing Editor:** Jo Finnis

**Editor:** Sue Wilkinson

**Design:** Barry Savage

**Photography:** Steve Tanner

**Illustrations:** John Smith

**Production:** Ruth Arthur; Neil Randles;
Karen Staff; Jonathan Tickner

**Production Director:** Gerald Hughes

DATE DUE